DATE DUE

Wisconsin

WISCONSIN BY ROAD

Celebrate the States

Wisconsin

Karen Zeinert and Joyce Hart

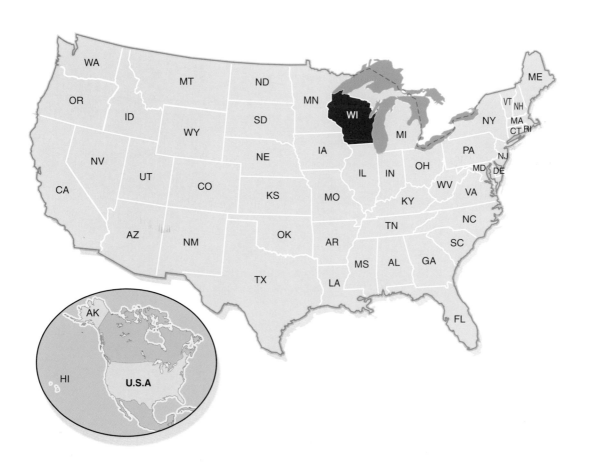

mc **Marshall Cavendish**
Benchmark
New York

Marshall Cavendish Benchmark
99 White Plains Road
Tarrytown, New York 10591-9001
www.marshallcavendish.us

All Internet addresses were correct and accurate at the time of printing.

Library of Congress Cataloging-in-Publication Data
Hart, Joyce, 1954–
Wisconsin / by Joyce Hart and Karen Zeinert.—2nd ed.
p. cm. — (Celebrate the states)
Summary: "Provides comprehensive information on the geography, history, wildlife, governmental structure, economy, cultural diversity, peoples, religion, and landmarks of Wisconsin"—Provided by publisher.
Includes bibliographical references and index.
ISBN-13: 978-7614-2157-3
ISBN-10: 0-7614-2157-2
1. Wisconsin—Juvenile literature. I. Zeinert, Karen. II. Title. III. Series.
F581.3.H37   2006   977.5—dc22   2005027379

Editor: Christine Florie
Editorial Director: Michelle Bisson
Art Director: Anahid Hamparian
Series Designer: Adam Mietlowski
Photo Research by Candlepants Incorporated

Cover Photo: SuperStock/age fotostock

Printed in China
1 3 5 6 4 2

Contents

People are drawn to this land . . .

"I consider the Wisconsin territory as so pleasant, so beautiful & fruitfull. The bear, the beaver, and the deer showed themselves to us often . . . indeed it was to us like a terrestrial paradise."

—French explorer Pierre Espirit Radisson

"British captain Peter Townsend wrote in his 1959 book, *Earth, My Friend*, that he had never breathed air so pure or been so comfortable with the scenery as he had been when he traveled in northern Wisconsin."

—journalist Jackie Loohaus, Milwaukee *Journal Sentinel*

. . . and they love its astounding wildlife.

"Wisconsin has played a major and highly visible part in the development of environmental protection in the twentieth century, including a key role in forming the national organizations of the Sierra Club and the Wilderness Society and in creating Earth Day in 1970."

—Wisconsin Historical Society

"On April nights, when it has become warm enough to sit outdoors, we love to listen to the . . . winnowing of snipe, the hoot of a distant owl, or the clucking of some coot."

—author and conservationist Aldo Leopold

"We see the wolves' tracks in the snow, hear their howls split the icy stillness of a moonlit January night. . . . It is so satisfying to know that they're here."

—editor Howard Mead

Wisconsinites tend to be a hardy, independent, creative breed . . .

"Cold weather here is something of a loyalty test, and enduring six months of it qualifies one as a local."

—teacher John Hildebrand

"Wisconsinites collect tales of the coldest, longest, and deepest winters."

—ecologist Inga Brynildson Hagge

"[They are people] to whom creed, color, race, money mattered less than [to anyone] I've ever encountered."

—Wisconsin novelist Edna Ferber

"Residents lay claim to the birthplace of the Republican Party, the Burlington Liars Club, and the Ringling Brothers Circus."

—writer William Curran

. . . with deep-seated enthusiasms.

"Listening to the people of Wisconsin is one of the most enjoyable parts of my job and a duty I take very seriously."

—U.S. Senator Russ Feingold

"They consider former Green Bay Packers coach Vince Lombardi a patron saint."

—Wisconsin journalist Tracy Will

Wisconsin is home to more than 5 million citizens. Wisconsinites are hardworking people who enjoy the beautiful surroundings of their state and see a bright future ahead. Let's take a closer look at Wisconsin to better understand how the land was formed, where its people came from, how its government was created, and what its people are doing today.

Chapter One

The Lay of the Land

The area now known as Wisconsin was largely shaped by fire, water, and ice. About one billion years ago, most of North America, including the area that is now Wisconsin, was perched on a red-hot mass of molten rock. As this huge mass expanded and pushed upward, it cracked the earth's crust in many places. Molten rock oozed through the openings. When the mass cooled, many new layers of rock were formed, some of which were rich in such metals as iron, copper, and lead.

More than 500 million years ago, the entire area was covered by a huge sea. Rivers from all over the land flowed into this sea and deposited sand. These deposits built up over thousands of years, and in the lowest layers pressure eventually fused the grains of sand together to create sandstone.

About one million years ago, four glaciers buried almost half of North America under tons of ice. These glaciers, as they moved farther south, reshaped the landscape, crushing and scouring the land underneath them as they went.

The great ice fields also leveled old deposits of molten rock and cut off the tops of ancient mountains, leaving Wisconsin relatively flat.

Once the bottom of an ancient sea, Perrot State Park formed millions of years ago as a result of accumulating mud, receding waters, and forceful glaciers.

These glaciers also dropped tons of gravel, soil, and boulders as they moved over the land. When they finally stopped, they left a huge moraine, or pile of dirt and rocks that had been pushed along in front of the mile-high ice field. Eventually the moraine became covered with vegetation. The highest elevation in Wisconsin, Timms Hill, is a bump on the long moraine, and today it is part of a thousand-mile-long hiking path called the Ice Age Trail. The view from the top is spectacular, especially in the autumn, when the maple trees covering the rolling hills below turn bright yellow, orange, and red.

Autumn fog lifts over Wisconsin hills.

When the glaciers finally began to melt about ten thousand years ago and to retreat northward, they scooped out enormous amounts of dirt in certain places, creating huge holes, which eventually were filled with the meltwater. Two of these large holes became Lake Superior and Lake Michigan. By the end of the glacial period, the land of present-day Wisconsin had over 15,000 lakes, 9,037 of which remain unnamed. Lake Winnebago is the largest one contained entirely within the state.

Meltwater also formed Wisconsin's vast system of rivers. These rivers rushed through the region, carving out deep valleys in the soft sandstone.

Point Beach State Forest is located along six miles of Lake Michigan's shoreline.

In the middle of the state the rivers flowed over flat areas and created marshlands. The longest of these rivers, the Wisconsin, cuts through the state for more than four hundred miles.

These marshes are very important to Ken Salwey. He is an environmental educator who is determined to protect Wisconsin's wetlands. To do this, he takes people on nature hikes so they can see the marshland's beauty firsthand. "Facts and statistics can only do so much," he said. "The heart and spirit have to be involved in learning to make it last."

When the glaciers melted, plants started to appear. Seeds buried beneath the ice sprouted when they were warmed by the sun. Other seeds were carried into the region by animals and wind. Eventually all of Wisconsin was carpeted with lush growth.

THE NORTHWOODS

The Northwoods area is located in the northern third of the state, which is divided into two distinct geographic regions: the lowlands near Lake Superior and the highlands where the ancient mountains had been. Both areas have shallow soil and good drainage—perfect places for trees to take root, especially pines. Ferns, fragrant blue violets, and snowy white trilliums sprout among the trees. Dotted among the pines are maples, beeches, aspens, birches, oaks, hickories, spruces, and hemlocks.

Such animals as elk, deer, rabbit, squirrel, bear, fox, lynx, marten, and wolf thrive in the Northwoods. The streams and lakes teem with fish, including twenty-foot-long sturgeon and muskellunge. According to frustrated modern-day fishers, ten thousand casts are required before one clever muskie is caught.

The Northwoods region is home to whitetail deer.

LAND AND WATER

Lake Superior

Superior

Ashland   Hurley

Namekagon R.   *L. Chippewa*

Rice Lake

Rhinelander

Mohawksin Lake

Menominee R.

St. Croix R.

Chippewa Falls

River Falls   Eau Claire

Chippewa R.

Black R.

Wolf R.

Marinette

Green Bay

Wausau

Big Eau Pleine Res.

Marshfield

Stevens Point

Green Bay

Michigan

Wisconsin Rapids

Appleton

Petenwell Lake

Lake Poygan

Lake Winnebago

Manitowoc

Mississippi R.

Tomah

Oshkosh

La Crosse

Castle Rock Lake

Fond du Lac

Sheboygan

Lake

Beaver Dam

Wisconsin R.

Madison

Milwaukee

Waukesha   West Allis

Mississippi R.

Janesville   Racine

Beloit

Kenosha

South of the Northwoods is the Central Plain. This area is sandy, flat, and in many places, wet. Tall grasses and bog plants, such as marsh marigolds, lotuses, and wild cranberries, grow there. Prairie grasses and purple asters thrive on the dry land; forests cover the rest.

Herds of buffalo once wandered the prairie. Fur-bearing animals seek shelter in Wisconsin's forests and marshes today, as do turtles, frogs, and migrating birds, such as sandhill cranes and trumpeter swans.

Sandhill cranes can be found wading in the tall grass of the Central Plain.

Like the Northwoods the southern part of the state is divided into two distinct regions that extend along Wisconsin's western and eastern borders. The glaciers stopped in the southeastern section of what would become Wisconsin. This region is now known as the state's Eastern Ridges and Lowlands. At one time the soil was very rich, and prairie grasses grew so tall and thick that they could completely conceal a standing person. Today most of this region consists of farmland, a few forested areas, some wetlands, and limited patches of the once vast prairie.

The southwestern section, which was untouched by the glaciers, is now known as the Western Uplands. This area is a dramatic mix of deep river valleys, and high sandstone bluffs. Grasses and wildflowers grow in the valleys, where cougars and rattlesnakes make their homes. This area is also the home of many birds, including the bald eagle. Each year in January, busloads of birdwatchers head to Prairie du Sac for Bald Eagle Watching Days, both to see the birds and to learn more about them at special lectures sponsored by the city.

PEOPLE ENTER THE LAND

The first people probably came to what is now Wisconsin about 12,000 years ago, just as the last of the ice age glaciers began to melt. Historians know very little about these ancient people. They do know that they were hunters whose ancestors probably came from Asia. Most were nomads who followed herds of animals as they migrated across the region.

Around 500 B.C.E. these native people began to settle in villages. They chose sites for practical reasons. For instance, some settled south of Lake Superior, near Lake Michigan, or along the area's many rivers.

Wisconsin's southwest region is one of high bluffs and fertile valleys.

These waterways made travel easier. Those who farmed settled in the south, since the long winters in the north made for a very short growing season. The soil was also better in the south.

The settlement pattern established by these first villagers was followed by the white people who began to arrive in the 1800s. In fact, this pattern is still followed today. More than two-thirds of Wisconsin's five million people live in the southern third of the state, and four of the state's five largest cities—Milwaukee, Madison, Green Bay, and Kenosha—lie near water, on the shores of Lake Michigan. Madison, the capital, lies in the middle of the state to make it more accessible to all state residents.

FOUR SEASONS TO ENJOY

Wisconsin's landscape is green and beautiful, but the climate can be harsh. As a northern state located in the upper Midwest, Wisconsin enjoys four very distinct seasons.

Summer and winter have the most extreme temperatures. Although a typical July day might be a moderate 70 degrees Fahrenheit, the temperature may soar to 100°F. The average temperature in January is 14°F. Spring and fall tend to be more comfortable, but Wisconsinites have to be ready for rapid changes in weather. In spring it is not unusual to have warm sunshine, a snowstorm, heavy rains, and blustery winds—all in the same week. Fall is a little more consistent, but snow flurries may appear as early as mid-October.

Wisconsin receives about 35 inches of precipitation per year, including meltwater from snow. Parts of northern Wisconsin may get as much as one hundred inches of snow during a really long winter, and snow can stay on the ground in the north for as long as 140 days.

Girls escape the heat during a scorching 100-degree day in Milwaukee.

Wisconsinites are known to complain about the weather, especially when they experience long bouts of bone-chilling winter temperatures that make their ears tingle and their eyes water whenever they step outside. For the Gunderson family of La Crosse, "summer never comes soon enough." On the other hand, a growing number of residents, especially those who like to ski and snowmobile, wish that winter would last even longer. The photographer Jeff Richter loves snow so much that he can watch it fall all week and not have his fill.

Children often look forward to a heavy snowfall or temperatures below −20°F. Travel then becomes so dangerous that the schools close, giving students a brief vacation. No matter what season a Wisconsinite

Wisconsin winters are cold and snowy—perfect conditions to build snowmen!

prefers, few deny that each time of year has its own beauty. A fresh snow-fall beneath a bright blue sky in January is quite a sight. And people look forward to wildflower displays in spring, a day at the beach in the summer, and eye-popping color in the fall, when the leaves turn brilliant shades of red, orange, and yellow.

CARING FOR THE ENVIRONMENT

Wisconsin's first settlers were awed by the beauty and wealth of resources they found there. John Muir, an immigrant from Scotland whose family moved to Wisconsin in 1849, wrote, "Oh, that glorious Wisconsin wilderness! Everything new and pure . . . flowers, animals, the winds and the streams and the sparkling lake. . . ."

Unlike Muir, who loved the beauty of Wisconsin's environment and became one of America's best-known conservationists, many other people who moved to Wisconsin believed that its resources were so abundant that they would never run out. As a result many people did little to protect the environment. Trappers killed every fur-bearing animal they could find. When they cleaned out the Northwoods, they moved into the marshlands of the Central Plain.

European settlers cleared and plowed under as much flat land as they could to create farms. When they had tilled all the fertile land on the prairie or in the valleys, they dammed up marshes to prevent rivers from entering them, drained the soil, and tried, unsuccessfully, to farm it. They also cut down forests. These actions destroyed thousands of acres of wildlife habitat. Meanwhile, loggers felled thousands of trees in the Northwoods to satisfy the growing demand for lumber. People everywhere polluted the rivers and lakes, and as manufacturing increased in the cities, the air became filled with soot and foul-smelling fumes.

Fortunately, not all Wisconsinites were willing to see their environment destroyed. As early as 1904, E. M. Griffith, the first person to be hired by the state to protect and expand the state's forests, set out to replant the Northwoods. Today Wisconsin has sixteen million acres of forested land, most of which is located in the northeastern part of the state. This represents 46 percent of Wisconsin's total land area.

The state and federal governments have also stepped in to control protected areas. The first state park in Wisconsin, Interstate State Park, located in St. Croix Falls, was formed in 1900. Today there are ninety-five state parks, forests, trails, and recreation areas in Wisconsin. State forests cover 490,000 acres. The vast majority of state forests are in the northern part of the state. Wisconsin's two national forests, Chequamegon and Nicolet, were merged into one in 1993. Together, they make up about another 1.5 million acres and are located in Wisconsin's Northwoods.

Aldo Leopold, known as Wisconsin's father of wildlife management, persuaded its citizens to further protect their environment. He began his crusade in 1930 by trying to set aside small, unused sites that could support plants and animals. He told Wisconsinites that "there are idle spots on every farm, and every highway is bordered by an idle strip. . . . Keep cow, plow, and mower out of these idle spots, and the full native flora . . . could be part of the normal environment of every citizen." People began to follow his advice, setting aside land on which plants and animals could live without being disturbed. In one case, after conservationists fought to preserve some marshland, Congress designated the area as a National Wildlife Refuge for migratory birds in 1941. This preserve, Horicon Refuge, is located in southeastern Wisconsin, close to Waupun. It has over 20,000 acres. Part of Horicon Marsh, the largest freshwater cattail marshland in the United States, is contained within the refuge.

Preservation of Interstate Park protects the billion-year-old geological formations there.

It is estimated that over one million Canada geese stop to rest and feed in this refuge during their long migration south in the fall and north in the spring.

Another place where wildlife is protected is in the Necedah National Wildlife Refuge, located in the Great Central Wisconsin Swamp. This refuge, which was created in 1939, is made up of over 43,000 acres and contains the largest wetland bog in the state. Over seven hundred sandhill cranes live in the refuge, which also provides a healthy environment for such endangered and threatened species as the massasauga rattlesnake and the Blanding's turtle. Other animals that live there include beavers, coyotes, gray wolves, and white-tailed deer. One of the main objectives of the refuge is to protect and restore the populations of whooping cranes and Karner blue butterflies. Both the cranes and the butterflies are endangered species.

As many as 200,000 Canada geese stop at the Horicon Marsh per day in the fall.

WHOOPING CRANES: A SUCCESS STORY

Whooping cranes were once near extinction. There was only one wild flock of whooping cranes left in the world. This flock of less than twelve pairs spent the warm months in Canada and the cold months in Texas. The International Whooping Crane Recovery Team, composed of American and Canadian scientists, was concerned about the flock being completely wiped out by a disease or by people polluting its habitats. These scientists decided that to save the whooping crane, they would have to establish another flock.

In the year 2000, in order to practice raising whooping cranes, the Necedah biologists practiced on sandhill cranes, raising them and then leading them in a lightweight aircraft on a new migration route that allowed them to spend the winter in Florida. At the end of April 2001, the sandhill cranes successfully returned on their own to Wisconsin. This flock became the first new migratory flock to be created.

In 2001, dressed in whooping crane costumes to make the young chicks think that the biologists were their parents, these scientists received ten whooping crane youngsters from Maryland, where they were raised in captivity. The biologists' job was to teach the cranes how to live on their own. While the chicks were too young to fly, the biologists (in their costumes) drove the lightweight aircraft on the ground so the chicks would learn to follow it. Then, when the chicks were ready to fly in October, the scientists led them to a winter home in Florida. In April 2002 five of the cranes flew over one thousand miles on their own and returned to Wisconsin.

Today, there are four generations of whooping cranes that fly to Florida from Wisconsin every winter and then return in the spring on their own.

Chapter Two

Settlement to State

Wisconsin's earliest settlers were part of a large cultural group that historians call the tribes of the Northeast Woodlands. These ancient people built villages south of Lake Superior. There they found copper in abundance, first in layers of rock close to the earth's surface and later in veins underground, which they mined. Archaeologists have found such copper artifacts as bracelets, rings, pendants, and beads. Copper tools, such as those used to punch holes, were also discovered.

MOUND BUILDERS

Besides being hunters, the first people to live in what is now called Wisconsin were also skilled craftspeople. Most of them settled near rivers throughout the southern half of the state. They built more than 15,000 earthen mounds, many of which still exist. Some of these mounds were round, others were shaped like upside-down cones. Most, though, were effigies built to resemble such animals as panthers, turtles, and eagles. The mounds were huge. Some that were shaped like eagles, for example, had wingspans of 1,000 feet, and those shaped like panthers had tails

This woodcut depicts a Native American on the shore of Lake Superior.

that were 300 feet long. Historians think these people built the mounds for religious reasons or as burial sites.

Researchers also believe that these mound builders were responsible for some impressive rock art in Wisconsin. This includes paintings (pictographs) on walls in sandstone caves as well as some carvings (petroglyphs) in the stone. Rock art was discovered in Wisconsin in 1878 in what is known as Samuel's Cave. Today there are two hundred known rock art sites in Wisconsin. Many are located in the southwestern portion of the state.

Some of the paintings, such as illustrations of hunting parties, are easy to understand. Others contain symbols, such as triangles with dots or pairs of wiggly lines, whose meanings are unknown. Petroglyphs and pictographs

Pictographs, such as this, have been found in many of Wisconsin's caves.

can be seen at the Wisconsin Historical Museum in Madison or at Roche-A-Cri State Park in Adams-Friendship.

These ancient people were not the only ones to build mounds in Wisconsin. About one thousand years ago, members of the Cahokia tribe, from what is now southern Illinois, migrated to Wisconsin to start a trading village on the Crawfish River. This group built earthen mounds that resembled the Aztec pyramids found in Mexico. Their village thrived for almost two hundred years before it disappeared. Historians and archaeologists are not completely sure how or why the Cahokia disappeared and are studying the ruins for more information. Today, Aztalan State Park, located halfway between Madison and Milwaukee, can be viewed by visitors, who are reminded that up until about 1200 C.E., this was a 21-acre, thriving city.

At the same time the Cahokia were building their village, other tribes, many of whom were farmers, settled in the southern part of Wisconsin. They raised corn, beans, squash, and tobacco in summer and hunted in winter. The Cahokia were the ancestors of some of the area's modern Native American tribes, such as the Winnebagos, Chippewa (or Ojibwa), Sioux (or Lakota), Ottawa, Potawatomi, and Menominee, as well as smaller groups. The Menominee tribe is the only group of Native Americans that has lived in Wisconsin continuously since ancient times. Their name refers to the wild rice they were known to gather and eat as a major part of their diet. They lived along the mouth of the Menominee River, near present-day Marinette. When French trappers arrived in the area, the Menominee people traded furs with them in exchange for guns, knives, clothing, and other wares. In 1854 the U.S. government created a reservation for the Menominee in northeastern Wisconsin on the Wolf River, where many of their descendants live today.

A Menominee village along the Menominee River

THE FRENCH ARRIVE

After Europeans found their way to North America, several nations sent explorers to the new continent. Among them was France. French explorers quickly realized that North America was extremely rich in fur-bearing animals. Shortly after, they built outposts in the American wilderness, and a thriving trade in pelts between the French and the Native Americans arose. French explorers ventured westward into the wilderness to find more people to trade with as well as a water passage that they hoped would eventually take them to Asia, where they believed untold riches could be found.

The best-known French explorer in Wisconsin was Jean Nicolet. He arrived at a narrow body of water (now known as Green Bay) in 1634 and was greeted by the Winnebagos. Nicolet was most interested in finding a water route to Asia, and he thought that the Native Americans could help him. But he was afraid that he would not be able to communicate with the native people, even though he had with him people who could speak and understand some Native American languages. So Nicolet decided to give the Native Americans a hint of what he was looking for by wearing a silk robe from China. He thought they would recognize the robe and point out the path to Asia.

Jean Nicolet was the first European explorer in the Great Lakes region.

Although the Winnebagos were impressed by Nicolet and his silk robe, they had no knowledge of a water passage to Asia. They tried to offset Nicolet's disappointment by promising to sell pelts to the French. They also held huge banquets for the explorer and his guides, and they invited all the Native Americans in the area to attend. This turned out to be a terrible mistake. Sadly, the French carried diseases against which the Native people had no immunity, and more than half of the Winnebagos became ill and died.

Later, French explorers were often accompanied by Jesuit priests who wanted to convert the Native Americans to Christianity. Father Claude-Jean Allouez was among the first priests to reach Wisconsin. He founded several outposts and a rustic mission near the Fox River in 1669. This mission was the site of Wisconsin's first permanent European settlement. It eventually became the city of Green Bay.

Heritage Hill State Historical Park, located near the original mission, contains a replica of the first chapel, which was made from bark, as well as a restored log cabin in which a fur trader lived around 1800. Each summer the park offers demonstrations about life on the Wisconsin frontier. Participants wear authentic costumes, use old recipes to prepare food over wood fires, and display old weapons.

The best-known French priest in Wisconsin was Father Jacques Marquette, who accompanied the French explorer Louis Jolliet in 1673. Jolliet was in search of a great river that Native Americans had often described. The two men and their guides sailed up the Fox River, one of the few in the state to flow northward, until they reached a swampy area and could go no farther. The local Native Americans then told the French to make a portage, or carry their boats, to the Wisconsin River, which was only a mile away. (Portage, Wisconsin, is located there.)

Father Jacques Marquette and explorer Louis Jolliet were the first Frenchmen to explore the Mississippi River.

Once the men reached the river, it was easy for them to sail downstream and into the mighty Mississippi River. With the discovery of the Mississippi, the French had the ability to go from Montreal, Canada, all the way to the Gulf of Mexico almost entirely by water. Marquette recorded the party's great discovery in his journal: ". . . we safely entered Missipi [*sic*] on the 17th of June, with a joy that I cannot express."

The French built a second settlement at the point where the Wisconsin River joined the Mississippi. This site was called Prairie du Chien (which means "prairie of dogs," the "dog" being a Native American chief who traded there). It became an important fur-trading center. The Fur Trade Museum, housed in the Brisbois store on St. Feriole Island, displays many artifacts from those exciting trading days.

QUILL ART

The Chippewas, also known as the Ojibwa, were a Woodland tribe of Native Americans who lived in the area that would become northern Wisconsin. They were known for their porcupine quillwork, a craft that required both patience and skill. After removing the long, supple quills from a porcupine—each porcupine has at least 30,000 quills the—Chippewas dyed them. They then worked the quills into baskets and clothing to add color and to create designs.

When other tribes saw the beautiful baskets, they wanted quills of their own. As a result, the Chippewas began to trade quills for other goods. Some of their best customers were Native Americans from the Great Plains, a place where porcupines were not found.

Today, the Chippewa continue to give demonstrations of their quill art at special craft shows and at powwows (dance festivals) held throughout the state. Most quill art is done on five reservations in northern Wisconsin, where more than 7,500 Chippewas still live.

THE ENGLISH TAKE CONTROL

In 1754 France and England began a battle over North America known as the French and Indian War. When it ended in 1763, victorious England received almost all of France's holdings in North America, including what would later be known as Wisconsin.

The English wanted peace with the Native Americans, most of whom had fought in the war on the side of their trading partners, the French. The English also wanted to buy pelts from the Native Americans. So the English decided to stop American colonists from moving into the Native American territory by outlawing settlement west of the Appalachian Mountains. This decision greatly upset the colonists and became one of the main causes of the Revolutionary War.

AN AMERICAN TERRITORY

The thirteen American colonies won their independence from England in 1783, when the war ended. In addition, they received all the land east of the Mississippi River. Because the western frontier was so far from the East Coast, Wisconsin was ignored for a while, and the French and the Native Americans in the area continued to trade as they had for many years.

However, new settlers began to move into Wisconsin in the early part of the nineteenth century. Some of them were miners. Lead was discovered in 1825 in the southwestern part of the state, at Mineral Point. Word of this find spread quickly, and miners from Missouri and other areas rushed in to make their fortune. Miners from as far away as Cornwall, England, also learned about the discovery of lead, and they, too, made their way to the Wisconsin wilderness. In 1825 there were only about one hundred miners in the area; by 1828 there were almost ten thousand.

The first miners were eager to get to work and unwilling to spend much time building shelters. They simply dug holes in the ground for homes and covered the openings with boards to keep out the rain. Because these holes were similar to those that badgers dig, the miners were called badgers. Eventually this nickname was applied to all Wisconsinites, and the state became known as the Badger State.

Vast improvements in transportation made what would become present-day Wisconsin easier to reach for would-be badgers. Canals and the invention of the steamboat made it possible to travel by water all the way from New York City to Wisconsin's east coast on Lake Michigan.

Steamships traveled along the Mississippi and Illinois rivers and entered Lake Michigan.

In addition, settling in the state was tempting because of the availability of cheap land. The government bought land from the Native Americans for as little as $0.17 per acre and then sold it to anyone who had the money for $1.25 an acre. This low price made it possible for families to buy large plots for farms and for other people to buy whole sections of land they hoped would become valuable sites for future cities. The lure of cheap land caused a land rush. In 1834 there were only two families in what is now Milwaukee. In 1835 there were more than 1,200 people living there. A journalist noted, "Every day, almost, new frames [for buildings] were erected."

The government offered cheap land that attracted homesteaders to Wisconsin.

The Winnebago chief Little Elk was amazed at the determination of the people of the United States to own so much land. He said, "The first white man we knew was a Frenchman. . . . He smoked his pipe with us, sang and danced with us . . . but he wanted to buy no land. The [Englishman] came next . . . but never asked us to sell our country to him! Next came the [American] and no sooner had he seen a small portion of our country, than . . . he wished us to sell it *all* to him. . . . Why do you wish to add our small country to yours, already so large?"

Even though Wisconsin's Native Americans were confused and upset by demands for their land, they seldom argued about selling it. They felt threatened by the white people and the large number of well-armed soldiers who were sent to the territory to protect the settlers. Eventually all of what is Wisconsin would be purchased from the local tribes, who would then be forced to live in poverty on the state's eleven reservations.

By 1836 the area out of which the state of Wisconsin would one day be created had enough people living in it to ask the U.S. government to declare the land an official U.S. territory. This would provide the people with special privileges as well as governmental protection for the residents of the new territory. At this time the territory's eastern boundary began west of the Mississippi River and included present-day Wisconsin, Minnesota, part of the Dakotas up to the Missouri River, and what would later become Iowa, where more than half of the population had built their homes.

Once Wisconsin became a territory, representatives from each county met to form a territorial government. The first legislators held their meetings in inns, which were much like today's hotels. Later, they built a temporary capital at Belmont. After many heated debates, Madison, which was conveniently located in the middle of the region, was chosen as the capital.

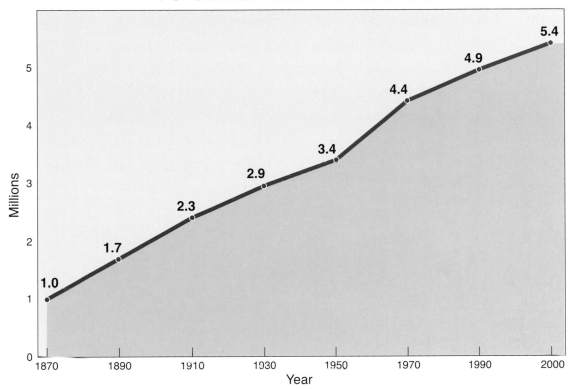

POPULATION GROWTH: 1870–2000

As soon as the territorial government was established, representatives began planning for statehood. They knew that as soon as the U.S. government recognized their territory as the state of Wisconsin, they would receive financial help for state improvements, such as new roads, railroads, and canals. Before all that could happen, though, there had to be at least 60,000 people living in the territory.

To reach the necessary number as soon as possible, recruiters set out to convince people to move to the area. These recruiters traveled to the East Coast and to Europe, promising people cheap land and a good living. They were so successful that by 1848 the territory had more than 200,000 people living in it. The population continued to grow at a rapid rate. Six years later the population had doubled. The new people came from nearby states, such as Missouri and Illinois, as well as many eastern ones, especially New York. Settlers also came from Germany, England, Ireland, Norway, Finland, and Switzerland. More people would immigrate to the region from such countries as Italy, Poland, and Czechoslovakia.

In order to attain statehood, the territory of Wisconsin needed more than 60,000 residents. Immigrants, as well as people living on the East Coast, moved to the area looking for cheap land and a better living.

Immigrants often wrote letters to friends and family members in their homelands encouraging them to move to Wisconsin. Among them was George Adam Fromader, from Germany, who settled in Jefferson in 1847. His first letter to friends was filled with encouragement and advice:

Anyone who has a desire to follow us may do so confidently if he can bring a little money along, whether it be a father or a family or a single person, man or woman. A skilled and industrious woman even though she brings no money into the country [for a dowry] may soon become a housewife. Women are highly respected in this country. . . . Whoever wants to make the trip need not bring a great deal except a supply of shirts and woolens. Do not bring tools of any kind, nor extra shoes, for the German ones are not worth carrying across the sea. No matter what you need or want, it is much better [here] than in Germany. The best route, also the cheapest, is via Bremen [a German port] and New York. The provisions to take on the trip are: good rye bread, cut small and toasted, oatmeal fried in lard, dried pork, dried noodles, coffee and sugar . . . dried prunes, salted butter, white hard tack. . . . You have no need for more advice, for I have told you all that is necessary.

Wisconsin's immigrants brought with them skills and a great desire to work. They were farmers, mechanics, craftspeople, teachers, traders, preachers, and politicians. All of them had something to offer and helped to make Wisconsin a great place to live.

HENRY DODGE: WISCONSIN TERRITORY'S FIRST GOVERNOR

Henry Dodge first arrived in what is now southwestern Wisconsin in 1827, where he settled—illegally—on Native American land. He brought with him his wife, nine children, some slaves, and a lot of experience in lead mining. The soon-to-become territory governor made a deal with the Winnebago tribe, and they helped him build a fort as well as a smeltery (a place in which lead is removed from rock).

In 1827 Dodgeville was founded. More than four thousand miners eventually joined Dodge, digging the lead out of the ground and making Wisconsin one of the world's leading producers. As more Europeans immigrated to the area to mine the lead, fights broke out with the Native Americans. Dodge helped to settle many of these disputes.

Then, in 1832, Dodge organized and headed a group of military volunteers that stopped a tribe of Native Americans, led by Black Hawk, who entered the territory in an attempt to reclaim land that had been taken away from them. After this bloody battle at Bad Axe, Dodge became regarded as a hero. Because of his bravery, President Andrew Jackson appointed Dodge as territorial governor of Wisconsin in 1836.

Dodge was not a typical governor. He always carried a bowie knife and often used foul language, which shocked ladies and even some gentlemen. Still, Dodge was an able governor, leading the first government in the territory and overseeing the committees that were selected to write a state constitution. After the territory became a state, Dodge was elected as one of Wisconsin's first U.S. senators, an office he held from 1848 to 1857.

In 1846 the population had increased to more than 60,000, and representatives from the territory asked the federal government to make Wisconsin a state. Congress agreed to do so, and on May 29, 1848, Wisconsin became the thirtieth state in the Union.

Wisconsin's representatives did not receive control over as much land as they had hoped. Lake Superior and Lake Michigan made natural borders for the state on the north and east. To the northeast was the state of Michigan and to the south was Illinois, borders that had already been drawn years before. So the people who lived in what would eventually become the state could only lay claim to what is Wisconsin today, plus some land to the west, which would eventually become Minnesota and Iowa. As a result Wisconsin was limited to 56,000 square miles. The federal government drew the state's western border along the Mississippi and St. Croix rivers.

BUILDING A MODERN STATE

The limit on land did not diminish Wisconsinites' desire to build a prosperous state. In fact, they set about their goal with even greater determination. One visitor from Ohio was amazed at the activity he saw in Milwaukee. He wrote, "A fellow can hardly get along the sidewalk. . . . Every kind of mechanism is going on in this place, from street hawking to manufacturing steam engines."

Wheat was the major crop then, but it wore out the soil quickly.

In 1846 Milwaukee was granted a city charter. Soon industry and businesses grew, attracting thousands of people.

And because wheat needed a long growing period, it could only be raised in the southern part of the state. On the other hand feed for cattle, primarily grass, grew all over the state. When the first cheese factory was built in Ladoga in 1864, it was very successful. Farmers then abandoned the plow for the cow, and a thriving dairy industry was born.

To help farmers and businesses get their products to market, state officials led the drive for the construction of better roads and new railroad lines. By the end of the nineteenth century Wisconsin had 6,000 miles of railroad tracks. It was then possible for farmers and businesspeople to ship their goods from almost anywhere in the state. Wisconsinites—two million of them by the turn of the twentieth century—could also live in any part of the state, not just in those areas that had good transportation.

First used to transport mined products, Wisconsin's railroad grew as agricultural products became the state's major industry and the need for transportation increased.

Many of the new businesses made wooden products from the tall pines harvested in the Northwoods. By 1900 Wisconsin led the country in the manufacture of wooden doors and wagons. The state would later become a major producer of wood pulp and paper products.

Although industrial growth has always been a major goal in the state, many Wisconsinites are no longer eager for more development. They worry that more industry and sprawling suburbs will harm the environment. Door County, located on the shores of Lake Michigan, has already decided to limit industrial growth. Said one county representative, "The time for action is now, while the county still has its charm." Two other counties in the state have followed suit.

The housing industry has become a threat to Wisconsin's farmland as more and more homes are built upon the land.

DRIVING SAW-LOGS ON THE PLOVER

Loggers were known as "shanty boys" because the cabins they lived in were called shanties. In this song the mother of a shanty boy is trying to discourage her son from continuing in this dangerous occupation. Surprisingly, he takes her advice. By the last verse he is telling other would-be shanty boys to stay at home on the farm.

"O Johnnie, I gave you schooling,
I gave you a trade likewise;
You need not been a shanty-boy
Had you taken my advice.
You need not gone from your dear home
To the forest far away,
Driving saw-logs on the Plover,
And you'll never get your pay.

"O Johnnie, you were your father's hope,
Your mother's only joy.
Why is it that you ramble so,
My own, my darling boy?
What could induce you, Johnnie,
From your own dear home to stray,
Driving saw-logs on the Plover?
And you'll never get your pay.

"Why didn't you stay upon the farm,
And feed ducks and hens.
And drive the pigs and sheep each night
And put them in their pens?
Far better for you to help your dad
To cut his corn and hay
Than to drive saw-logs on the Plover,
And you'll never get your pay.

A log canoe came floating
Adown the quiet stream.
As peacefully it glided
As some young lover's dream.
A youth crept out upon the bank
And thus to her did say,
"Dear mother, I have jumped the game,
And I haven't got my pay.

"The boys called me a sucker
And a son-of-a-gun to boot.
I said to myself, 'O Johnnie,
It is time for you to scoot.'
I stole a canoe and started
Upon my weary way.
And now I have got home again,
But nary a cent of pay.

"Now all young men take this advice;
If e'er you wish to roam,
Be sure and kiss your mothers
Before you leave your home.
You had better work upon a farm
For half a dollar a day
Than to drive saw-logs on the Plover,
And you'll never get your pay."

Chapter Three

Wisconsinites Are . . .

Wisconsinites come from many different places and bring with them a variety of different lifestyles. Native Americans were the first to settle in the area. Then came people from such European countries as Germany and Switzerland. As time passed, people who lived in such places as Laos and Vietnam made their homes in Wisconsin. More recently, immigrants from Mexico and other Spanish-speaking countries have found Wisconsin a good place to work and raise their families. When people come to live in new places, they bring parts of their native culture with them. This means that today in Wisconsin, visitors can sample various types of Asian food. They can hear traditional Mexican music. They can learn about people from all over the world without ever leaving the state.

. . . A RACIAL AND ETHNIC MIX

In the first part of the nineteenth century, most people in Wisconsin were Native American. That has changed dramatically over the years. Today, out of a total population of five million, only 47,228 are Native American. Approximately 4,769,857 are white, 304,460 are black, and 88,763 are Asian.

Wisconsinites take great pride in their diversity, heritage, and culture.

More than half of the state's Asians are Hmongs, an ethnic group from Laos who actively supported the United States during the Vietnam War. The Hmongs were forced to flee their homeland when the United States withdrew from Asia at the end of the Vietnam War. Wisconsin is home to one of the country's largest concentrations of Hmongs.

Although only 3.6 percent of Wisconsinites are Hispanic, their number is growing faster than that of any other group. Some of them are former migrant workers who decided to stay after coming to Wisconsin to help harvest farm crops.

A young Asian girl celebrates her heritage at the Independence Day festival.

ETHNIC WISCONSIN

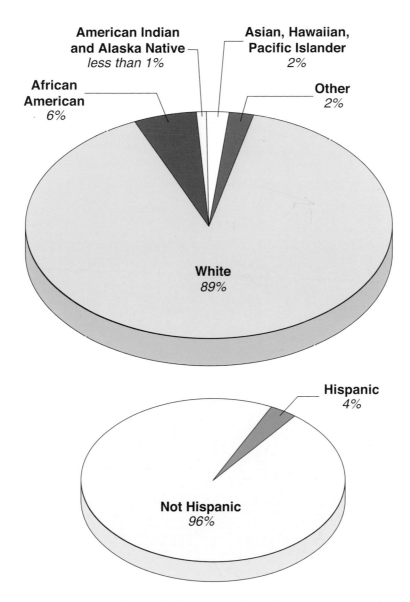

American Indian and Alaska Native
less than 1%

Asian, Hawaiian, Pacific Islander
2%

African American
6%

Other
2%

White
89%

Hispanic
4%

Not Hispanic
96%

Note: A person of Cuban, Mexican, Puerto Rican, South or Central American, or other Spanish culture or origin, regardless of race, is defined as Hispanic.

Wisconsinites love to celebrate and hold festivals to honor the many ethnic groups that live in the state. They also get together to celebrate at harvesttime. And if they want to throw a party but lack a reason, they invent one. As a result, Wisconsin has some rather unique events, including a cherry pit-spitting contest in Fish Creek.

German Fest, the largest festival of its kind in North America, is held in Milwaukee during the summer. Bands play polkas, craftspeople demonstrate their Old World wares, and workers in food tents struggle to keep up with the demand for wurst (sausage), soft pretzels, and beer. These three days of singing, dancing, and fellowship are called *Gemütlichkeit* in German.

Wisconsin's Germans celebrate during the German Fest parade.

Instead of statewide festivals, Hmong communities hold smaller annual celebrations scattered across Wisconsin. Most of these are held on the Hmong new year, which usually falls at the end of November. Events include dance performances, guitar playing, and games, such as *pov bob*, a ball game played among young single adults as part of a courtship ritual. Usually, festivals include displays of intricate needlework, including appliqué, delicate beadwork, and items decorated with hundreds of tiny stitches. Many needlework projects are quilts that picture Hmong villages or illustrate historical events. Many Hmong take part in the Asian American Summer Festival held each year in Madison, where visitors can watch traditional dances and hear Hmong songs. "It's a good way to learn about the Hmong culture," said Thaj Ying Lee, the executive director of United Refugee Services of Wisconsin.

Various Native American tribes also hold festivals—called powwows—in Wisconsin. Twenty-two-year-old Thirza Defoe, of the Oneida tribe, performs in many of these celebrations. Part of her demonstration includes a traditional hoop dance, during which she twirls twenty-four hoops at one time. She learned how to do this dance in a Native American school in Milwaukee. She was chosen to dance at the opening ceremonies of the Barcelona Olympics in 1992 and has danced in countries around the world.

At the Indian Summer Festival, Native Americans celebrate with singing and dancing.

Not all celebrations are ethnic in nature, though. Wisconsinites love to eat, and they often celebrate when crops are harvested. There are so many of these festivals that it is hard to keep track of them all. Terese Allen toured the state while writing a book about the state's food festivals. She identified three hundred. She knew about the strawberry, apple, cherry, and mustard festivals. "But," she added, "I was amazed to learn there's also events that feature rutabagas, cucumbers, sauerkraut, Armenian lamb stew, bluegills, ginseng, and pea soup."

More than 100,000 people attend the Sweet Corn Festival, where almost 70,000 tons of corn are served.

ROSEMALING

Wisconsin's many ethnic festivals often showcase special crafts. Norwegian celebrations feature rosemaling, the art of decorating objects with intricate designs, including painted flowers, leaves, and scrolls.

Hundreds of years ago some painters in Norway made a living by traveling from home to home, decorating cupboards and wooden chests. The designs were often unique to a particular area or valley, and art experts today can tell where an artist came from by examining his or her designs. Although rosemaling flourished for many years, it went out of style in the late nineteenth century.

Interest in the craft was revived in Wisconsin by Per Lysne of Stoughton. Lysne had long admired old rosemaling designs and set out to duplicate them in the 1930s. He began by decorating some wooden plates and cupboards for friends. Word of his artistic ability spread, and soon others were asking him to do work for them. As more and more people saw Lysne's designs, they became interested not only in the artist but in the art itself. As a result, others took up rosemaling. Today, several community colleges offer classes in this craft.

Although Wisconsinites can be expected to attend festivals in huge numbers, when it comes to voting, they are unpredictable. They do not consistently support any one political party. They might elect a Republican governor and a majority of Democratic representatives to the state assembly. On the other hand, they have been known to repeatedly reelect candidates they like. For example, Tommy Thompson, a Republican, held the office of governor from 1987 until 2001. Senator Gaylord Nelson served in the U.S. Senate for eighteen years, between 1963 and 1981. Before that, he was the governor of Wisconsin.

Over the years Wisconsinites have elected representatives with very different political beliefs. In the early 1900s Wisconsinites supported candidates known as Progressives, who promised to change government and make it more responsive to the people. Government, they believed, could solve problems.

By the mid-twentieth century many Wisconsinites no longer trusted political leaders, especially on the federal level. They believed that government not only couldn't solve problems, but had become a problem in itself. Full of doubt and mistrust, the voters sent Joseph McCarthy, a new man on the political scene, to the U.S. Senate in 1947.

McCarthy became one of the state's most controversial senators. He believed that the federal government had been infiltrated by Communist spies who were plotting to destroy the country. He set out to expose them. When some Americans cheered him on, McCarthy, who was politically ambitious, made many accusations. "This caused headlines all over the country," he said later, "and I never expected it." To keep up the attacks, McCarthy decided that he might need some actual evidence. He asked friends to help him find it.

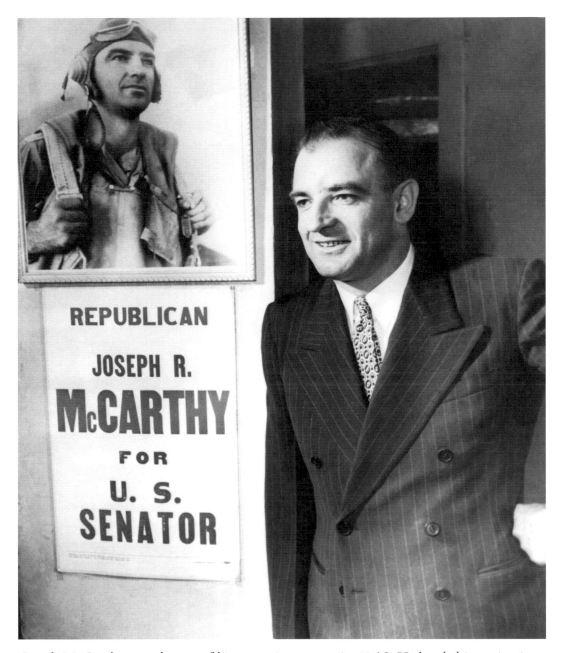

Joseph McCarthy poses by one of his campaign posters in 1946. He headed investigations into Communist influences in the U.S. government.

His investigations grew increasingly wild and irresponsible, and he accused many innocent people. Because of McCarthy, many people lost their jobs. Some Wisconsinites were so embarrassed and so upset with McCarthy that in 1954 they tried to recall him, or force him to run in a special election before his term was up. This attempt failed. But by then the American public was tiring of McCarthy's antics and began to ignore his usually unfounded charges.

FLAG DAY

The first Flag Day was celebrated at Stony Hill School near Waubeka, Wisconsin, on June 14, 1885. The school's teacher, Bernard Cigrand, had been looking for a way to show how much he loved his country. He finally established a day to honor the flag.

Cigrand was determined to have Flag Day celebrated across the country. He repeatedly asked the government to proclaim June 14 a national holiday. Finally, in 1916, President Woodrow Wilson and Congress agreed to do so.

Today, many communities host Flag Day parades. The largest is held in Appleton, Wisconsin.

POPULATION DENSITY

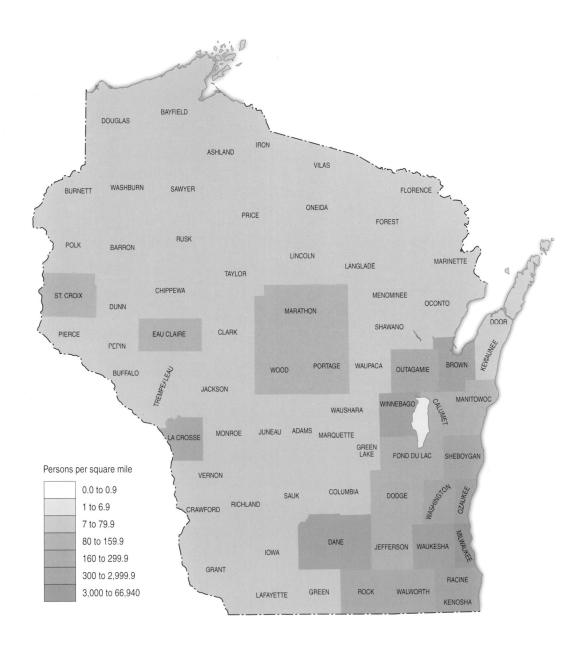

Persons per square mile

- 0.0 to 0.9
- 1 to 6.9
- 7 to 79.9
- 80 to 159.9
- 160 to 299.9
- 300 to 2,999.9
- 3,000 to 66,940

DOUGLAS
BAYFIELD
ASHLAND
IRON
VILAS
BURNETT
WASHBURN
SAWYER
FLORENCE
PRICE
ONEIDA
FOREST
POLK
BARRON
RUSK
MARINETTE
LINCOLN
LANGLADE
TAYLOR
ST. CROIX
CHIPPEWA
DUNN
MENOMINEE
OCONTO
EAU CLAIRE
CLARK
MARATHON
SHAWANO
PIERCE
PEPIN
DOOR
KEWAUNEE
BUFFALO
WOOD
PORTAGE
WAUPACA
OUTAGAMIE
BROWN
TREMPEALEAU
JACKSON
MANITOWOC
WAUSHARA
WINNEBAGO
CALUMET
LA CROSSE
MONROE
JUNEAU
ADAMS
MARQUETTE
GREEN
LAKE
FOND DU LAC
SHEBOYGAN
VERNON
COLUMBIA
DODGE
WASHINGTON
OZAUKEE
CRAWFORD
RICHLAND
SAUK
DANE
JEFFERSON
WAUKESHA
MILWAUKEE
IOWA
GRANT
RACINE
LAFAYETTE
GREEN
ROCK
WALWORTH
KENOSHA

On the whole Wisconsinites have been eager to shoulder their responsibilities as U.S. citizens. More than 90,000 men from the state fought for the Union during the Civil War. Wisconsinites also served in every other war and military action in which the United States has been involved.

That does not mean that Wisconsinites have always agreed on participating in these wars, though. During the Civil War some German immigrants resented being drafted to fight for the Union. Many had fled their homeland in order to avoid forced military service. Similarly, many Wisconsinites of German decent opposed the United States' involvement in World War I as an enemy of Germany. One of the state's two senators and nine of its eleven representatives voted against entering the war. In the early 1970s some college students at the University of Wisconsin in Madison led demonstrations against the United States' participation in the war in Vietnam. Some of these demonstrations erupted in violence.

. . . ENTHUSIASTIC SPORTS FANS

Wisconsinites might disagree about politics or whether the country should enter a war, but few argue about enjoying sports. Most residents like to hunt, fish, snowmobile, cross-country ski, swim, hike, or cheer their favorite professional sports teams. These teams include the Milwaukee Bucks (basketball), the Milwaukee Brewers (baseball), and the Green Bay Packers (football). Before the Brewers, the Braves represented Milwaukee in baseball's major leagues. Led by Hank Aaron, the greatest home-run hitter in baseball history, the Braves won the World Series in 1957. When the Bucks won their only National Basketball Association championship in 1971, they were led by basketball's all-time greatest scorer, Kareem Abdul-Jabbar.

Of all the professional sports teams in the state, the Packers are the most popular. Fans have been particularly loyal since the 1960s, when Vince Lombardi was the coach, and the Packers won the first two Super Bowl games (1967 and 1968). Even though the Packers failed to return to the Super Bowl for twenty-nine years, fans still filled the stadium for every game to cheer on the team.

Green Bay Packers fans show their support during the 1997 Super Bowl.

When the Packers finally reached the Super Bowl in 1997, fans went wild. Hundreds purchased plane tickets to New Orleans, where the game was played, just to greet the team when it arrived. Thousands went to the game. And while the Packers were pitted against the New England Patriots, the streets of Wisconsin were deserted. It seemed as though everyone was glued to their television sets. When the players returned to Green Bay victorious, the city held a huge welcome-back parade for the champions. Schools were closed so that children could join the celebration.

It is no surprise, then, that such a popular team has produced its share of heroes. Among them is Brett Favre, a three-time winner of the NFL's Most Valuable Player award. Favre has been such a positive influence on the Green Bay Packers' success in recent years that he was given a lifetime contract with the team, the first person ever granted that honor by the Packers. In 2004, after Favre played in his two hundredth consecutive game, the governor of Wisconsin declared November 29, 2004, as Brett Favre Day. Favre is the only professional athlete in any sport who has started every game his team has played over a fourteen-season period. But it is not just his consistency in showing up for games that makes him great. He has a good arm, something very important for a quarterback. He was recently clocked releasing the ball in 1.4 seconds, an astonishing feat. Over his career Favre has won a lot of awards, including being chosen to play in the Pro Bowl eight times.

Brett Favre throws for the Green Bay Packers early during the 2005 season.

Chapter Four

Governing Wisconsin

As the United States was developing as a country, every territory had to write its own constitution in order to become a state. But Wisconsin's constitutional committee faced an especially difficult task in doing so. It needed to write a constitution that would satisfy many different ethnic groups, some of whom could not speak to each other because they did not share a common language. It also had to design a state government that would be strong enough to hold these groups together, settle disputes when they arose, and provide a way to let people govern themselves on a local level so that their specific needs could be met.

INSIDE GOVERNMENT

The Wisconsin constitutional committee organized the state government in 1848, which is still much the same as it was when it was developed.

Executive

The executive branch is headed by the governor. This branch has other officers as well: a lieutenant governor, an attorney general, a state treasurer, a secretary of state, and a superintendent of public instruction.

A mural depicting the scales of justice decorate the state capitol building in Madison.

Governor Jim Doyle addresses the legislature during his State of the State address.

All of these officers are chosen by voters through statewide elections. Rarely are all of them from the same political party. As a result political clashes in the executive branch are not unusual.

Officials in the executive branch have two jobs. They make sure that the state's laws are executed, or carried out. They are also responsible for identifying problems in schools, society, or the economy, for which they must find solutions.

Legislative

The legislative branch has two bodies, the senate and the assembly. The state is divided by population into thirty-three districts, and citizens in each district elect one representative to the state senate and three representatives to the assembly. The legislature drafts bills that become law if they pass both bodies and are signed by the governor. It also decides the state's taxes to be collected and how that money is spent.

Judicial

The judicial branch tries people accused of crimes and settles disputes. This branch consists of three kinds of courts: circuit courts, courts of appeal, and a supreme court. The seventy circuit courts are the first to hear cases. The court of appeals listens to pleas from people who have lost their cases in circuit courts. The Wisconsin Supreme Court is the court of last resort; it hears pleas from people who have lost their first appeal if it believes that justice might not have been served. This court has seven justices.

Built between 1906 and 1917, Wisconsin's state capitol is designated a National Historic Landmark.

It is currently headed by Chief Justice Shirley Abrahamson, the first woman to serve as chief justice.

Judges are elected by the residents of Wisconsin. Circuit and appeals court judges are elected by people in the district in which they serve, and supreme court justices are selected through statewide elections. Unlike other elected state officials, judges may not campaign as members of a political party, nor can they discuss how they would vote on a particular issue, should it come before the court. Voters are instructed to select judges based on their ability to make good decisions, not on their beliefs.

Chief Justice Shirley Abrahamson was appointed to the supreme court in 1976. Her term will end July 2009.

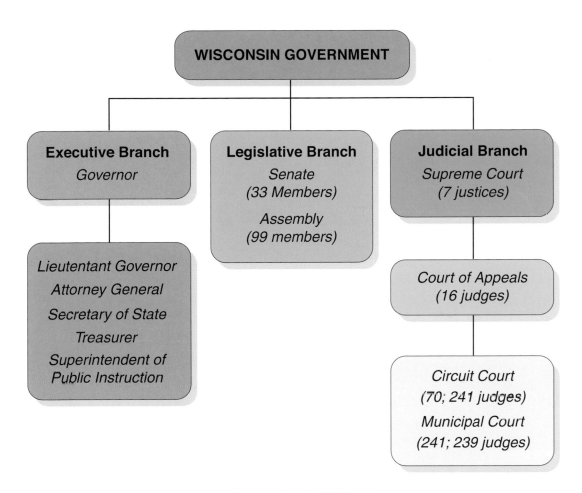

WISCONSIN GOVERNMENT

Executive Branch
Governor

Lieutentant Governor
Attorney General
Secretary of State
Treasurer
Superintendent of Public Instruction

Legislative Branch
Senate (33 Members)

Assembly (99 members)

Judicial Branch
Supreme Court (7 justices)

Court of Appeals (16 judges)

Circuit Court (70; 241 judges)
Municipal Court (241; 239 judges)

PROBLEM SOLVING

Wisconsin's government works well. Even so, the state has problems to solve. When Jim Doyle was elected as Wisconsin's forty-fourth governor in 2003, he said there were three areas he wanted to focus on: making sure that children were well provided for in education and health care, helping Wisconsin's economy grow, and finding good, renewable energy sources.

Education

Wisconsin's first public school opened its doors in 1845 in Southport (now called Kenosha). Four years later Wisconsin's public school system opened statewide. By 1879 all children were required to attend school through the eighth grade.

Today students must remain in school until they graduate high school or until the end of the term during which they turn eighteen years of age. The only ones who do not have to follow this law are children who belong to the Amish community. The Amish are members of a religion that rejects all modern conveniences, such as electricity. Amish children are often needed at home to help their parents, so they are allowed to finish their education after they have completed the eighth grade.

Education has always been important to the people of Wisconsin. The first German immigrants to arrive in Wisconsin, for instance, brought with them a tradition of private education. Some of these immigrants started their own schools, and they established the first kindergarten in the United States. Other Wisconsinites started private schools as well, most of which were run by Protestant churches or Catholic parishes. Today, there are about 990 private schools in Wisconsin with about 139,455 students. About another 878,809 students attend the 2,180 public schools in the state.

One of Governor Doyle's most important programs, called KidsFirst, was established in 2004. The main goal of this program is to make sure that all Wisconsin's children received a good education. As Governor Doyle has said, "Wisconsin's future depends on the success of our children today."

The KidsFirst program has provided money to allow more children to attend preschool and kindergarten classes. The aim of the program is to develop the reading skills of very young students so that their education in elementary school will be improved. By teaching all children to read in kindergarten, Governor Doyle hopes fewer Wisconsin students will drop out of school before they graduate high school. If students are good readers, they have a better chance of learning and will therefore get better grades in school.

All of Wisconsin's children are required to attend school through twelfth grade. These Hmong students are just a few of the eight hundred Hmong that attend Wisconsin's schools.

Governor Doyle also believes that the KidsFirst program will encourage more young Wisconsinites to continue their education after high school by attending college. In college the students will gain professional skills by studying math, computer science, and other subjects so that when they graduate they will be able to use their skills to improve the state. All this begins with a good early education program. The KidsFirst program has caught the attention of governors in other states, who are observing the progress and improvement in Wisconsin schools.

One of Governor Doyle's main goals is the education of Wisconsin's children. Governor Doyle said, "I promised myself if I ever became Governor, I would make Wisconsin's children my number one priority."

MARGARETHE SCHURZ'S KINDERGARTEN

In 1852 Margarethe Schurz and her husband, Carl, left Germany for the United States, where they first settled on the East Coast. They soon decided to move westward. They chose Wisconsin as their destination, and in 1856 they arrived in Watertown, a small town in the southern part of the state.

While Carl busied himself with political issues, Margarethe turned her attention to children, whom she loved dearly. She decided to open a school for four and five year olds. The school followed an education system that she had observed in Germany. Margarethe called her school "kindergarten" (which means "a garden of children" in German). It was a place where students learned to socialize with one another, sing, dance, and play games. Margarethe's kindergarten helped to prepare her students for first grade. Her schools became so successful that the idea spread throughout the nation, and today almost all school systems in the United States include kindergarten.

ECONOMIC GROWTH

Traditionally, Wisconsin's economy has depended largely on the land. Most of the state's land is devoted to farms and forests. Wisconsin's farmland provide such agricultural products as milk and cheese, which are sold all over the United States. From the forests, trees are cut and used to make wood products, such as lumber and paper. Another part of Wisconsin's economy depends on the manufacturing sectors, which produce such things as food products, tools, furniture, and automobiles.

Although these play an important part in Wisconsin's economy, recent changes in the United States and in the world, such as the high cost of oil and the outsourcing of jobs (using factories in other countries to make products that people in the United States buy and use), has made people in Wisconsin think about other ways of making money. Residents have concluded that it is very important to provide training and additional education to every citizen in the state. Offering specialized training after high school will give Wisconsin a skilled workforce that will be able to handle new types of jobs, such as those in technical fields. In addition, state officials and people involved in business are working to attract new industries to Wisconsin to provide jobs for the people who graduate from college. This will mean that college graduates will not have to leave the state to find employment.

Wisconsin is dedicated to educating its youth in all sectors. Here, a student is learning how to test water quality.

WISCONSIN BY COUNTY

Another area in which Wisconsin has been a leader in the United States is in energy conservation and finding renewable energy sources. Only about 4 percent of the energy the state uses comes from renewable sources. Most energy analysts believe that Wisconsin can increase this level to 10 percent by the year 2015.

Using renewable sources of energy might include burning corncobs to produce energy. It is easy to grow more corn each year. On the other hand, coal, oil, and natural gas, which are in limited supply and cannot be created each year, are nonrenewable energy sources. If the state relies too heavily on these fossil fuels for energy, one day there might not be enough to go around. Wind is also a renewable source of energy. Wind is constantly being created by different climate changes. Another renewable source is the sun. Solar panels can be placed on the roofs of buildings, for example, and the energy captured by the panels can be used to generate electricty.

Solar panels on this roof will transform energy from the sun into electricity.

Wisconsin pays over $6 billion to import oil from other countries each year. Wisconsin can save money by finding more renewable sources of energy and can also improve the quality of the air by burning materials that cause less pollution.

NATIVE AMERICAN RIGHTS

When different cultures live in the same area, conflicts sometimes arise. This has been true in Wisconsin ever since pioneers began moving into territories where large tribes of Native Americans had lived since ancient times. Some of these differences have been settled through treaties, or official agreements, between the two groups of people. But treaties have often been broken. Today Wisconsinites, both Native American and whites, continue to work together to help solve their disputes. Some of the concerns that are being discussed in Wisconsin today include fishing rights and the use of Native American images and names as mascots for sports teams in schools and other places.

When Native Americans sold their land, the state gave them permission to fish without limit on public lands and lakes. This caused controversy among non-Native people, who had to limit the number of fish they caught. Some non-Native Wisconsinites thought it was unfair that Native Americans could catch as many fish as they wanted. Many people were also afraid that Native Americans might catch all the fish there were in Wisconsin's rivers and lakes, leaving none for other people. However, Wisconsin's courts upheld the Native Americans' right to unlimited fishing, and eventually everyone came together to address conservation issues. Today Native Americans, sportsmen, and environmentalists are working together to preserve Wisconsin's wildlife and natural heritage for everyone to enjoy.

A Native American fisherman uses a handmade fishing net to catch fish in Lake Superior.

Another issue that is causing some debate involves the use of Native American names and images as mascots. Many schools in Wisconsin use references to Native Americans in their sports teams, with such terms as Redmen, Red Raiders, Indians, or Blackhawks. Native American groups began protesting the use of words that refer to their culture in a demeaning or stereotypical way as early as the 1960s. But it was not until 1988 that Wisconsin schools began to acknowledge the protest and start doing something about it. In that year twenty-one schools decided to stop using the references.

In 1994 Wisconsin's Department of Public Instruction strongly suggested that all the state's schools discontinue the use of Native American images and names. Slowly but surely, more and more of Wisconsin's schools are changing any reference to Native Americans that is considered insulting. There is a slogan on a Native American Web site that states, "Indians are people, not mascots." By banning these names, Native Americans hope the non-Native people of Wisconsin will stop seeing them as cartoon characters or as threatening figures.

Native Americans from Wisconsin protest the use of Indian mascots.

Chapter Five

Making a Living

In recent years Wisconsin has had one of the lowest costs of living in the United States. This means that not only can people find jobs in the state, but many people can also afford to buy nice cars and homes.

In 2004 the average income per person was $32,157. This is close to the national average of $32,937, which is a good indication that Wisconsinites are enjoying fairly comfortable lives.

Helping to maintain this strong economy are the many schools in the state that offer a good education, which allows students to graduate with skills they can use to earn a good salary. Wisconsin's high schools also have the third-lowest dropout rate in the United States. This means that Wisconsin's students are studying hard and Wisconsin's teachers are doing a good job of preparing their students for the future.

To further educate its students, Wisconsin has developed one of the world's leading centers for research and development in the growing field of biotechnology at the University of Wisconsin. Wisconsin has also created a technical college system with sixteen different locations throughout the state. These schools provide vocational education and

Wisconsin enjoys a low cost of living and low unemployment. Here a farmer and his son harvest cranberries.

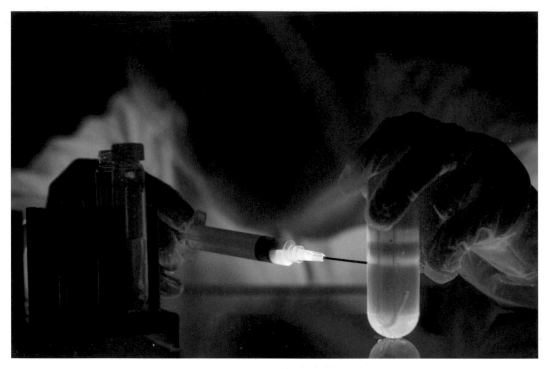

Research and development is a growing field in Wisconsin.

extra training after high school to help Wisconsinites gain skills so they can find better-paying jobs.

Most workers in Wisconsin are employed in agriculture, manufacturing, and the service sector, which includes trade and tourism. Over 400,000 people work for the government. The industries in the state with the largest numbers of employees were businesses that produce dairy products, cars and other motor vehicles, paper, meat products, and small engines. Most businesses are located in or near the largest cities, such as Milwaukee, Madison, and Green Bay.

If a person was looking for a job in 2005, two of the best fields to find one were nursing and manufacturing. There was a great need for nurses in private practices as well as in Wisconsin's hospitals. There were also a lot of jobs for machinists, especially those who work with metal and plastic products. Other jobs that were most available were teaching in preschools and working in other child care services, such as day care centers. The best places to do business, according to one study, were in Green Bay and in Madison, which were ranked as the top two best midsize cities in which to work in the United States.

During 2005 manufacturing was one of the best fields to find a job.

2004 GROSS STATE PRODUCT: $212 Million

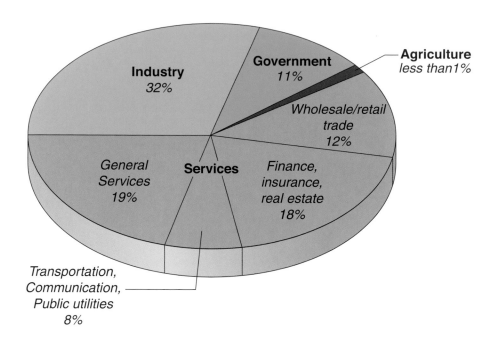

Industry
32%

Government
11%

Agriculture
less than1%

Wholesale/retail
trade
12%

General
Services
19%

Services

Finance,
insurance,
real estate
18%

Transportation,
Communication,
Public utilities
8%

AGRICULTURE

The number of farms in Wisconsin has decreased over the years. In 2004 there were only 76,500 working farms listed in the state. Most of Wisconsin's farms (99 percent of them) are still family owned. Even though farmers make up only a small part of Wisconsin's entire workforce of over three million people, they produce so many crops that they have a significant effect on the economy. The net farm income for 2005 was projected to be between $1.2 and $1.5 billion.

One product that comes from Wisconsin's farms is milk. Today there are over 1.2 million cows in the state, which produce 13 percent of all the milk in the United States—enough to furnish every American with a quart of milk every week. But not all of this milk is used as a beverage.

Wisconsin corn growers harvest almost four million acres of corn each year totaling almost $1 billion.

More than 17,000 dairy farms operate in Wisconsin.

Some of it is turned into butter, cheese, and other dairy products. Wisconsin ranks second (California ranks first) among the states in the production of milk and butter. That's why Wisconsin is often called America's Dairyland.

Jeff Pollack is a young, successful dairy farmer. His 365 cows produce 24,000 pounds of milk each day. Pollack is optimistic about the future of his farm and proud of the cheese he makes. "Dairy farming is in good shape," he said. "Things are looking up. Our cheese could go up against any. A lot of places don't have good quality cheese."

Some of Wisconsin's most plentiful crops are snap beans, peas, beets, and cranberries. It is also one of the top producers of sweet corn, cucumbers for pickles, cabbage for sauerkraut, and potatoes for chips and frozen fries.

Other farm products include maple syrup, honey, apples, and cherries, as well as beef cattle, hogs, and chickens.

Perhaps the state's most unusual farm product is ginseng. This root crop is in great demand in the Far East, where it is used in medications. Ginseng is a fussy plant that is difficult to grow; it needs an acidic soil, shade, and perfect drainage. It also grows slowly. It cannot be harvested until it is at least three years old. This is one of the reasons ginseng root sells for about $50 per pound in Asia. Wisconsin's Marathon County, in the middle of the state, is the nation's leading ginseng producer. One farmer recently harvested more than 300,000 pounds of ginseng root!

The best of Wisconsin's agricultural products are put on display at the state fair, which is held each year in West Allis. Fairgoers often begin their day by examining displays of some of the biggest tomatoes, the reddest homemade strawberry jam, and the tastiest cherry pies. They then can go to the barns to see some of the best cows, pigs, sheep, geese, ducks, and rabbits in the state. Most of these animals were raised by children. Fairgoers also watch tractor pulls and horseback-riding competitions. And they might sample freshly roasted corn on the cob and as many rich cream puffs—a fair specialty—as their stomachs will allow.

The perfect soil and weather conditions in Wausau make it the capital of the U.S. ginseng industry.

CHERRY CRISP

Cherries have been an important ingredient in eastern Wisconsin dishes for many years. Below is a simple recipe for a scrumptious dessert called cherry crisp.

Crust:
1 stick butter, melted
1 cup brown sugar, packed
1 cup flour
1 cup quick-cooking oatmeal
1/4 teaspoon each baking powder, salt, and baking soda
Pinch cinnamon

Filling:
2 cups pitted tart cherries (fresh, or frozen, thawed, and drained)
3/4 cup cherry juice or water
1/4 to 1/2 cup sugar (sweeten to taste)
3 tablespoons cornstarch
1/8 teaspoon almond extract

Mix all ingredients for crust except cinnamon. Pat half of this mixture into a 9 x 9 x 2 inch pan. Blend cornstarch, sugar, and liquid in saucepan over medium heat. Bring contents to a boil, then simmer, stirring constantly, until mixture thickens. (Ask an adult to help you.) Add almond extract and cherries. Pour filling over crust. Sprinkle the remaining crust mixture over the filling. Top with a sprinkling of cinnamon. Bake in a 350°F oven for 30–35 minutes. Serve warm or cold, with or without vanilla ice cream.

WISCONSIN WORKFORCE

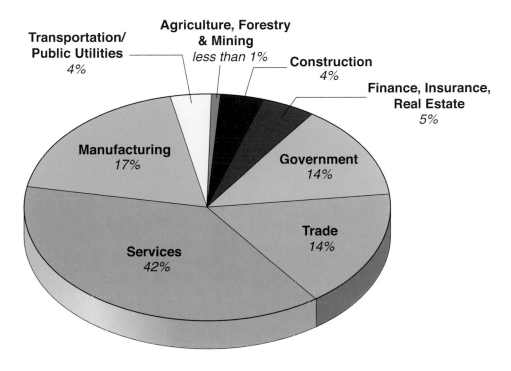

Transportation/ Public Utilities *4%*

Agriculture, Forestry & Mining *less than 1%*

Construction *4%*

Finance, Insurance, Real Estate *5%*

Manufacturing *17%*

Government *14%*

Services *42%*

Trade *14%*

INDUSTRY

Fewer jobs with manufacturing firms have been available in Wisconsin in recent years, as manufacturing companies have left the United States to take advantage of the cheaper labor available in other countries. However, many Wisconsinites still rely on manufacturing jobs to make a living.

People who work for manufacturing firms make products from local raw materials or from imported goods. In total, Wisconsinites manufacture products worth more than $36 billion each year. Among the best known companies are Oshkosh B'Gosh clothing, Oscar Mayer hot dogs, Frito-Lay snacks, J. I. Case tractors, John Deere snowmobiles, Mercury Marine outboard motors, Harley-Davidson motorcycles, Rayovac batteries,

The Harley-Davidson plant, outside of Milwaukee, manufactures components for their Sportster and Buell models.

paper products such as Kleenex, submarines for the government, and yachts for the wealthy.

Perhaps one of the best-loved products made in the state is manufactured by a small company called Foamation, which makes funny foam hats shaped like a wedge of cheese that sports fans wear to baseball and football games. Chris Becker, the general manager of the company, said that he has shipped "cheeseheads" all over the world. "We've had calls from Germany, Japan, and the Netherlands." Sue LeMay, a receptionist who has handled many requests for the product, adds, "People are just fascinated with these cheeseheads."

A young "cheesehead" proudly wears her cheesehead hat, manufactured in Wisconsin.

EXPORTS

Wisconsinites make more products than they can use, so much of what is made is shipped to other states and countries. In 2004 Wisconsin businesses shipped out more than $12 billion worth of products. Wisconsin's largest international market is Canada. Canadians bought almost $5 billion worth of Wisconsin products. Other large markets for Wisconsin's goods are Mexico, China, Great Britain, Germany, France, Belgium, Australia, and South Korea.

Computers and computer equipment are some of the best-selling export items. Other popular items include transportation equipment, paper products, and electrical equipment and appliances.

EARNING A LIVING

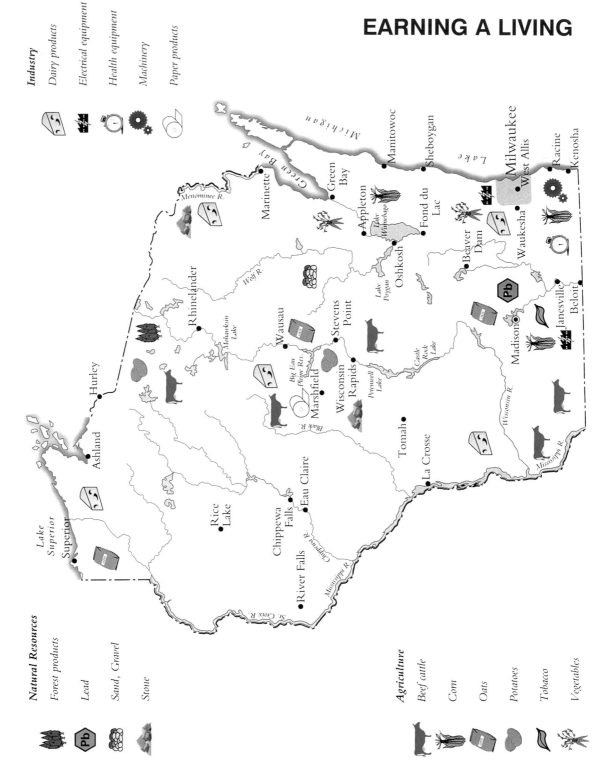

Industry

Dairy products
Electrical equipment
Health equipment
Machinery
Paper products

Natural Resources

Forest products
Lead
Sand, Gravel
Stone

Agriculture

Beef cattle
Corn
Oats
Potatoes
Tobacco
Vegetables

THE SERVICE SECTOR

The service sector, the largest employer in the state, includes jobs that help the people of Wisconsin in many different ways. Wisconsinites working in the service sector include those who work in hospitals, in grocery stores, and in hotels, just to name a few. About 312,900 Wisconsinites earn their living by selling Wisconsin-made products or imported goods. About another 58,200 workers are employed by trucking and warehousing firms, which transport and store these goods. Other service businesses include banks, real estate agencies, insurance firms, and communications companies, restaurants, and the tourism industry.

About ten million tourists visit Wisconsin each year. For most of these visitors the Wisconsin outdoors is the great attraction. Many visitors take advantage of Wisconsin's state parks. In them they can hike trails, bike country roads, catch some of the sixty million fish taken yearly from state waters, ski, snowmobile, hunt, shop, or just plain relax in the warm Wisconsin sun. While visiting the state, tourists help Wisconsin's economy. By spending money at hotels, restaurants, and tourist attractions, these visitors help to pay for the salaries of people who work in these places. Over the course of one year, tourists spend over $11 billion in Wisconsin. To encourage even more tourists to visit, Wisconsin has adopted the slogan "WI Life's So Good" as the theme of an advertising campaign that is shown across the nation.

Tourists enjoy a ride through the Dells on the Wisconsin River.

Chapter Six
"WI Life's So Good"

First-time tourists in Wisconsin are often surprised by the state's varied landscape. These visitors expect to see little but thousands of acres of farmland. Although Wisconsin certainly has many beautiful farms, it also has other sights worth visiting. As the state's ads say, "WI Life's So Good." Visitors can take in the sights, one region at a time.

THE EASTERN LOWLAND AND RIDGES

There is much for tourists to see in Milwaukee, the largest city in the state. The Milwaukee County Zoo, among the most highly rated zoos in the country, has over 2,500 animals and birds. Lucky visitors can take short rides on camels or elephants. Those who prefer more traditional means of getting around can tour the grounds in a "zoomobile," which offers a guided tour of the zoo.

Milwaukee is also the home of the Mitchell Park Horticultural Conservatory. This building has three seven-story-tall glass domes that house tropical, desert, and flowering plants. The tropical dome contains jungle plants, including orchids, and many birds, especially tiny finches. The desert dome

A kayaker explores the Apostle Islands National Lakeshore.

A model train is set up in the floral dome of the Mitchell Park Horticultural Conservatory.

houses many cacti and tall palm trees. The floral show dome houses seasonal shows. One of the best-attended displays is the Christmas exhibit, in which thousands of red poinsettias and Christmas trees covered with tiny twinkling lights fill the dome with color and fragrance.

Milwaukee has many other forms of entertainment from which to choose. Sports fans can catch a Brewers baseball game or Bucks basketball game, depending on the season. Music fans can attend a performance by the Milwaukee Symphony or take in a concert by a well-known celebrity at the Marcus Center for the Performing Arts. In addition, visitors can attend any number of festivals that are held in the city.

Some restaurants and shops specialize in ethnic foods, especially German dishes, and many visitors enjoy sampling European-style cooking. Usinger's meat market sells sixty kinds of sausages, many of which are made from old German recipes.

Just southwest of Milwaukee, near Eagle, is Old World Wisconsin. This unique museum has sixty barns, homes, and stores that were built by some of the first European immigrants to arrive in the state. These buildings were moved from their original locations to the museum's grounds. Buildings that were too large to be moved in one piece were taken apart and then reassembled when they reached Eagle.

Old World Wisconsin is an outdoor educational site that re-creates pioneer life in Wisconsin.

Madison is also a popular tourist destination. The state capitol building is a smaller version of the national capitol building located in Washington, D.C. Wisconsin's capitol is made from marble and granite to ensure that it will not be destroyed by fire, as an earlier structure was in 1904. The building is topped with a high dome. Inside, the dome is decorated with an elaborate painting that shows the many natural resources of Wisconsin. Guides give tours (more than 70,000 people go through the building each year), and if the legislature is holding a public debate, visitors are welcome to observe.

Downtown Madison is filled with an unusual blend of historic buildings and modern city designs. On Wednesdays and Saturdays in the summer and fall, farmers bring in truckloads of tomatoes, melons, and sweet corn to sell on the capital's sidewalks. Opposite this rural scene are some of the trendiest art galleries and clothing stores in the state. Nearby, the Wisconsin Historical Society gathers information from the past, while just down the street, 41,000 University of Wisconsin students learn skills to prepare for the future.

About 80 miles northeast of Madison is Oshkosh. Oshkosh is the home of the Experimental Aircraft Association, which draws thousands of people from all over the world to its Fly-In each summer. While the Fly-In is going on, the Oshkosh airport is one of the busiest in the world. Owners of experimental airplanes meet to share their love of flying and to learn new techniques for building better planes. Aircraft used in World Wars I and II as well as huge jets, such as the Concorde, appear in special programs, as do daredevil stunt pilots. Throughout the year visitors can watch films about experimental aircraft in the AirVenture Museum's auditorium and look at numerous planes and aviation displays in several different buildings.

State Street is the heart of downtown Madison, where great sites, sounds, and tastes can be explored.

All of Door County, the thumblike peninsula that juts into Lake Michigan, is a tourist destination. In the spring seven thousand acres of flowering cherry trees and one million daffodil bulbs put on a colorful show. In the summer tourists visit lighthouses, relax on sandy beaches, catch big fish in Lake Michigan, and hike the many trails in four state parks. The county is also home to many artists, and visitors can watch potters and painters at work and buy original works of art in local galleries.

In addition, Door County restaurants offer some tasty treats. Almost every eatery offers some kind of cherry dessert: pies, cobblers, or crisps, which are topped with rich vanilla ice cream. When visitors want something more substantial than dessert, they head to restaurants that serve fresh fish cooked over wood fires.

The Wisconsin Point Lighthouse sits at the end of a 3-mile pier at the entrance to Superior Harbor.

TEN LARGEST CITIES

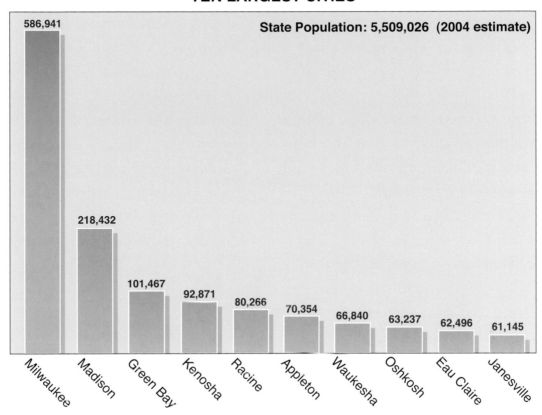

State Population: 5,509,026 (2004 estimate)

City	Population
Milwaukee	586,941
Madison	218,432
Green Bay	101,467
Kenosha	92,871
Racine	80,266
Appleton	70,354
Waukesha	66,840
Oshkosh	63,237
Eau Claire	62,496
Janesville	61,145

THE NORTHWOODS

One of the best-known towns in the Northwoods is Peshtigo. By 1871 most of the nearby area had been cleared of trees, and acres of old stumps and piles of pine needles baked dry by a summer drought surrounded much of the village. On October 8, 1871, when a small fire grew out of control, the blaze spread rapidly. Fanned by high winds, the flames roared through the village so quickly that eight hundred residents were killed within minutes. The roaring fire continued on its path of destruction, burning a swath forty miles long and ten miles wide in only four hours. In all, 1,200 people were killed.

The Peshtigo Fire Museum tells the dramatic story of America's greatest fire disaster.

Hayward is another Northwoods community with an interesting history. Like Peshtigo, this town was once surrounded by logging camps. The men who lived there worked from dawn to dusk. The work was so strenuous that few of them remained loggers for more than a couple of years. To pass the long nights away from their friends and families, they sang songs and made up tall tales about life as a lumberjack. Today, Hayward's attractions include shows about what skills were needed to be a lumberjack long ago.

Equally popular are the many crystal-clear lakes in the area. The bottoms and shores of these lakes are covered by sand so fine that it is called sugar sand. Families often rent cottages there for a week or two to swim and fish.

When the fish are not biting, disappointed anglers can visit the National Fresh Water Fishing Hall of Fame in Hayward. The four-story museum is shaped like a giant muskie, one of the state's most popular fish.

Hayward is also a popular winter spot for visitors who like to snowmobile or ski. The Birkebeiner, the largest cross-country ski race in the country, is held near Hayward. More than eight thousand participants enter this race every year.

North of Hayward is Pattison State Park, where Big Manitou Falls is located. At 165 feet, Big Manitou is the highest of the area's many waterfalls.

Skiers from around the world gather in Hayward for North America's largest cross-country ski marathon.

Bayfield, on the shores of Lake Superior, is the gateway to the Apostle Islands, the northernmost point in the state. Tourists can catch ferries there to visit the twenty-two islands, including Madeline Island, the only one of the Apostles with year-round residents. These residents are thought to be some of the hardiest in the state. When ferry service stops in late fall, the islanders are isolated until the lake freezes solid between Madeline and Bayfield. Islanders can then drive their snowmobiles or cars over the ice to the mainland.

The beautiful Apostle Islands have been designated as part of a national lakeshore. The red of the rock, caused by iron in the stone, against the bright blue waters of the world's largest freshwater lake makes a colorful picture.

The fishing in this area is great. Lake trout, perch, and pike are abundant. Commercial guides take fishers to the best spots, making it nearly impossible for any angler to end the day empty-handed.

During winter, Apostle Island's sea caves freeze, creating dramatic ice formations.

THE HORRIBLE HODAG

One of the most entertaining of Wisconsin's tall tales comes from the Northwoods. It is the tale of the Hodag, which Gene Shepard (1854–1923), a prankster, supposedly stumbled on in 1893 in the woods near Rhinelander. This animal, according to Shepard, breathed fire and posed in a menacing fashion. The creature, he told everyone who would listen, was mean, *really* mean.

To capture the Hodag, Shepard enlisted the help of friends who were known to wrestle bears for fun. The men tiptoed to the Hodag's den and stuck a long pole topped with a chloroform-saturated rag into the cave. The strange creature was overcome by the chloroform fumes and passed out. As soon as it was safe to do so, the men rushed in, bound the Hodag, and took it to Shepard's place.

Word spread about the Hodag. To accommodate everyone who wanted to see it, Shepard took his discovery to county fairs, where he allowed a few people at a time to enter his dimly lit tent for a quick peek. People were awestruck by the alligatorlike critter, which had two horns on its head and twelve spikes running down its back. Some spectators were even frightened when the animal began to move toward them.

Eventually, everyone heard about the Hodag, thanks to articles about it that appeared in many newspapers. When word reached the Smithsonian Institution in Washington, D.C., scientists there announced that they were heading to Rhinelander to study the animal. Shepard then had to admit that the whole thing was a joke. The Hodag that people had seen was made of wooden parts that moved when Shepard pulled some wires.

Today, a statue of the Hodag stands on the outskirts of Rhinelander. It is the mascot of the city and a reminder of one of Shepard's most successful pranks.

PLACES TO SEE

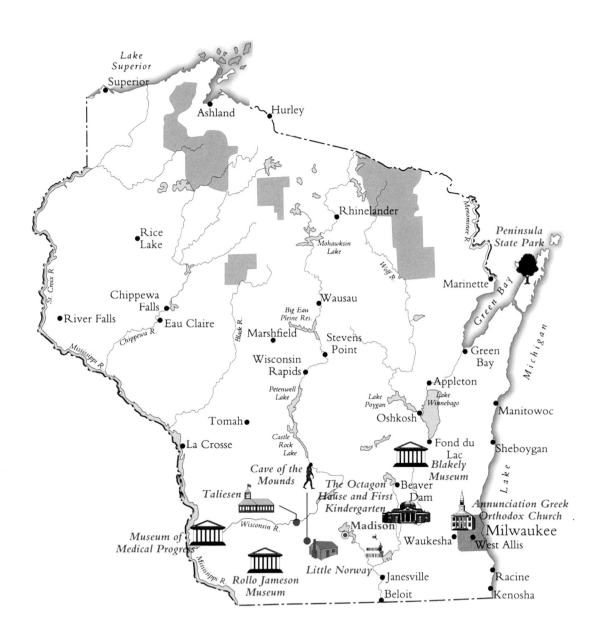

Lake
Superior

Superior

Ashland • Hurley

Rhinelander

Rice
Lake

Mohawksin
Lake

Peninsula
State Park

Menominee R.

Marinette

Chippewa
Falls

Wausau

Big Eau
Pleine Res.

Wolf R.

Green Bay

•River Falls

Eau Claire

Chippewa R.

Marshfield

Stevens
Point

Green
Bay

St. Croix R.

Black R.

Michigan

Mississippi R.

Wisconsin
Rapids

Lake
Poygan

Lake
Winnebago

Appleton

Manitowoc

Tomah•

Petenwell
Lake

Oshkosh

Castle
Rock
Lake

Fond du
Lac

Sheboygan

•La Crosse

Cave of the
Mounds

Blakely
Museum

Taliesen

The Octagon
House and First
Kindergarten

Beaver
Dam

Annunciation Greek
Orthodox Church

Lake

Museum of
Medical Progress

Wisconsin R.

Madison

Milwaukee
West Allis

Mississippi R.

Rollo Jameson
Museum

Little Norway

Waukesha

Janesville

Racine

Beloit

Kenosha

The wetlands, sometimes called the Great Swamp of Wisconsin, dominate the Central Plain. Wildlife thrives there in a national preserve as well as in state refuges. The Sandhill Wildlife Area becomes a temporary home for at least five thousand sandhill cranes in October, when the birds seek a safe resting place on their annual southward migration.

Nearby, cranberries are grown in huge bogs. When the fruit is ready for picking, tour buses loaded with visitors eager to attend local cranberry festivals and watch workers harvest the fruit arrive. By this time the berries are floating on top of water that has been forced into the bogs to separate the berries from their plants. Workers "rake" the berries together and put them into containers. Once the fruit is cleaned and packaged, it is sent all over the country.

Cranberries are Wisconsin's number one fruit crop, growing on more than 100,000 acres.

On the southern edge of the Central Plain lie the Wisconsin Dells. According to Native American legend, the Dells' 7-mile-long canyon was carved out by a huge serpent that moved southward through the area. Scientists believe that water from the last of the ice age glaciers began to create this canyon about 12,000 years ago. When the glacier thawed, some of the meltwater was dammed up behind rocks, creating a huge lake. Eventually, the water broke through the natural dam and rushed southward, sculpting a new riverbed and the Dells. Over the years water, wind, and frost have sculpted the soft sandstone into strange formations. These formations have been given descriptive names, such as the Beehive and the Grand Piano.

Most visitors tour the area, which is divided into the Upper and Lower Dells, on amphibious vehicles called "ducks" that are half boat and half bus. Others take in the sights by strolling along boardwalks that meander through places such as Cold Water Canyon, a good place to be on a hot summer day.

Northwest of the Dells, Mill Bluff State Park contains more unusual rock formations. The pillarlike shapes were once islands in the glacial lake. Water wore away the softest stone over thousands of years. Today, visitors can imagine what the islands looked like thousands of years ago.

Mill Bluff is now part of the Ice Age National Scientific Reserve. The reserve has nine sections that outline the edge of the last glacier. Currently, Wisconsin is purchasing land and developing a hiking trail that will connect these sections. The final trail will be

Formed millions of years ago, the forces of nature are still changing the Dells today.

more than 1,000 miles long, enabling hikers to see firsthand the effects that the glacier had on the state.

The Western Uplands is edged on the west by the St. Croix and Mississippi rivers. Scattered along the waterways, especially the Mississippi, are many small towns. Most were built in tiers on the steep bluffs that face the river. Some of the oldest buildings—former banks, feed mills, and bars—have been restored. They now serve as art shops and quaint restaurants.

Most visitors tour the area by following the Old River Road, Highway 35. Others take paddle-wheel boat tours on the Mississippi or rent a houseboat and spend a week or two on the river.

Small villages in the center of the region are full of surprises. An old flour mill in Augusta reminds visitors more of New England than of Wisconsin. The Norske Nook, a café in Osseo, serves the most famous pies in the state.

Many cheese factories in the southern part of the Uplands sell cheddar, Colby, Swiss, and Limburger, as well as cheese curds made fresh each day.

Two of the best-known homes in the state, Taliesen and the House on the Rock, are located near Spring Green. Taliesen was once the home of Frank Lloyd Wright, a world-famous architect from Wisconsin. Wright believed

Built along the Mississippi River, Fountain City is the oldest town in Buffalo County.

that buildings should blend into their surroundings. Therefore, many of his designs, like Taliesen, were no taller than the surrounding trees, and most were made from local stone and wood.

The House on the Rock was built by Alex Jordan. This house, according to local rumors, was built to outdo Wright's Taliesen. Jordan's house is set partially on top of a large sandstone rock and partially in the rock itself. Large portions of the walls are carved out of the stone, as are the stairs and some of the benches and tables. But spectacular as it is, the house is not the main attraction. Beneath the house is a maze of rooms filled with an incredible variety of items, including clocks from Germany, ships in bottles, old dentistry tools, antique cash registers, whole storefronts that were typical of Main Street shops years ago, and a gigantic merry-go-round. In short, the House on the Rock has something for everyone—a lot like Wisconsin itself.

Frank Lloyd Wright began building Taliesen in 1911. His revisions lasted until his death in 1959.

THE FLAG: *The state seal appears in the center of the flag. The word "Wisconsin" is at the top of the flag. The year Wisconsin became a state, 1848, appears under the shield. The flag was adopted in 1913, and the name of the state and the date of statehood were added to the flag in 1979.*

THE SEAL: *A sailor and a miner support a shield with symbols for agriculture, mining, shipping, and manufacturing. Wisconsin's loyalty to the Union is symbolized by a small U.S. coat of arms. A badger sits above the shield and represents the state's nickname, the Badger State. The state seal was adopted in 1881.*

State Survey

Statehood: May 29, 1848

Origin of Name: A word derived from a Native American language, which may have several possible meanings, including "gathering of the waters"

Nickname: The Badger State

Capital: Madison

Motto: Forward

Bird: Robin

Animal: Badger

Fish: Muskellunge

Insect: Honeybee

Flower: Wood violet

Tree: Sugar maple

Rock: Red granite

Fossil: Trilobite

Mineral: Galena

Badger

Honeybee

ON, WISCONSIN!

The music for "On, Wisconsin!" was composed in 1909 and entered in a Minnesota contest for the best new football song. Instead, the composer was persuaded to dedicate it to the University of Wisconsin football team. In 1913 lyrics better suited to a state song were added. Although "On, Wisconsin!" was recognized as Wisconsin's song for many years, the state did not officially adopt it until 1959.

Words by

J. S. Hubbard and Charles D. Rosa   Music by William T. Purdy

Highest Point: 1,952 feet above sea level, at Timms Hill

Lowest Point: 581 feet above sea level, along the shores of Lake Michigan

Area: 54,314 square miles

Greatest Distance North to South: 310 miles

Greatest Distance East to West: 260 miles

Bordering States: Upper peninsula of Michigan to the north, Illinois to the south, Iowa and Minnesota to the west

Hottest Recorded Temperature: 114°F, at Wisconsin Dells, July 13, 1936

Coldest Recorded Temperature: −54°F, at Danbury, January 24, 1922

Average Annual Precipitation: 20 inches

Major Rivers: Bad, Chippewa, Fox, Iron, La Crosse, Manitowoc, Menominee, Milwaukee, Mississippi, Montreal, Oconto, Rock, St. Croix, Sheboygan, Wisconsin, Wolf

Major Lakes: Big Green, Geneva, Mendota, Monona, Pepin, Poygan, Winnebago

Trees: aspen, beech, birch, hemlock, hickory, maple, oak, red pine, spruce, white pine

Wild Plants: black currant, blueberry, fern, huckleberry, Juneberry

Animals: bear, beaver, coyote, deer, fox, gray wolf, raccoon, skunk, woodchuck

Birds: chickadee, coot, duck, goose, grouse, jacksnipe, loon, partridge, pheasant, quail, robin, swallow, warbler, wren

Fish: bass, muskellunge, pike, perch, sturgeon, trout, walleye

Endangered Animals: barn owl, Blanchard's cricket frog, Canada lynx, ornate box turtle, peregrine falcon, skipjack herring, slender glass lizard, timber wolf, trumpeter swan, yellow-throated warbler

Endangered Plants: brook grass, Carolina anemone, chestnut sedge, mountain cranberry, Lake Huron tansy, pinedrop, rough white lettuce, sand violet, spotted pondweed, wild petunia

Woodchuck

Barn owl

700 C.E. Mound builders construct effigies in the area.

800–1600 The Winnebago, Ottawa, Sioux, and Chippewa arrive in Wisconsin.

1634 Jean Nicolet becomes the first known white man to reach Green Bay.

1637 Father Marquette and Louis Jolliet arrive in Wisconsin.

1763 Wisconsin becomes part of British territory.

1783 Colonies gain independence from Britain; Wisconsin becomes part of the United States.

1848 Wisconsin becomes the thirtieth state.

1851 First state fair is held; The first railroad, which runs from Milwaukee to Waukesha, begins service.

1854 The Republican Party is founded in Ripon.

1861–1865 About 90,000 Wisconsinites fight for the Union during the Civil War.

1868 Christopher Latham Sholes patents the first typewriter.

1871 Peshtigo fire kills 1,200 people.

1884 Ringling Brothers Circus is founded in Baraboo.

1890 Dr. Stephen Babcock develops a test to measure the butterfat content of milk.

1900 Robert M. La Follette is elected governor, the first governor to have been born in the state; population of the state reaches two million.

1917 Present capitol building is completed in Madison.

1931 Wisconsin enacts the nation's first state unemployment compensation law.

1946 Joseph McCarthy is elected to the U.S. Senate.

1967–1968 Green Bay Packers win the first two Super Bowls.

1970 Earth Day is founded by the Wisconsin senator Gaylord Nelson.

1972 Milwaukee Brewers baseball team is founded.

1982 Milwaukee Brewers win the World Series.

1996 Shirley Abrahamson becomes the first woman to hold the office of chief justice of the Wisconsin Supreme Court.

1997 Green Bay Packers win the Super Bowl.

2001 Timber wolves are removed from the endangered species list.

2003 Jim Doyle is sworn in as Wisconsin's forty-fourth governor.

2004 Forty-five whooping cranes return to Wisconsin after wintering in the South.

ECONOMY

Agricultural Products: apples, barley, cranberries, dairy products, green peas, livestock, oats, potatoes, snap peas, soybeans, sweet corn, wheat

Manufactured Products: automobiles, electrical equipment, machinery, medical supplies, paper products, plumbing fixtures, processed foods

Natural Resources: basalt, clay, gravel, iron, lead, quartzite, rich soil, sand, sandstone, zinc

Business and Trade: finance, insurance, real estate, retail, tourism

CALENDAR OF CELEBRATIONS

Northern Exposure Family Festival/Wolf River Rendezvous In January visitors can enjoy the brisk air of winter while watching top sled dog racers from Europe, Canada, and the United States compete in this three-day event in Shawano.

Apples

World Championship Snowmobile Derby More than three hundred professional snowmobile racers from all over the world compete for the world championship and other prizes at Eagle River in mid-January.

Hudson Hot Air Affair Over forty hot air balloons compete in this race held every February over the St. Croix River valley near Hudson. Watch a torchlight parade during which the balloon pilots and crews light up the darkness with fire from their balloon baskets.

Snowflake International Ski Jumping Tournament Westby, the U.S. home of ski jumping, hosts world-class jumpers during this February contest. The five ski jumps in Westby are used to train Olympic hopefuls.

Sons of Norway Barnebirkie Birkebeiner hosts America's largest cross-country ski event for children in February. More than 1,700 children, ranging in age from three to thirteen, participate.

Door County Festival of Blossoms Visitors can enjoy a magnificent view of more than one million daffodils, wildflowers, and tulips in early May. Visitors can also enjoy boat tours of several lighthouses.

Syttende Mai In May Stoughton honors its Norwegian heritage with the longest-running Norwegian Independence Day festival held outside of Norway. There's plenty to do, including parades, folk dancing, an ugly troll contest, and arts and crafts.

Hot air balloons

Inland Sea Kayak Symposium This annual conference is held in Bayfield/Washburn in June and celebrates nature and its valuable resources. Attendees can learn about camping or ecosystems, or join one of twelve kayak excursions.

Summerfest Visitors who like music should be sure to stop in Milwaukee for this eleven-day festival, which runs from late June to early July, to hear music and watch professional athletes give demonstrations.

NFL Training Camps/"The Cheese League" Football fans get a treat in July when several NFL teams delight spectators with scrimmages and exhibition games in "Cheese League" towns: Platteville, La Crosse, River Falls, and Green Bay.

German Fest An oompah band and classical musicians liven up Milwaukee in July. This is the largest German festival of its kind, and it offers tuba playing contests, fireworks, and plenty of German food.

Lumberjack World Championship Even though this is a professional contest, amateurs can enjoy the fun at this Hayward event held every July. Kids can enter logrolling events, and adults can chop and saw their way to prizes.

Experimental Aircraft Association International Fly-In The world's largest aviation event takes place every July and August in Oshkosh at Wittmann Regional Airport. More than 11,000 airplanes—all sizes, shapes, and types—come from around the world. Visitors can learn the history and mechanics of flight.

Experimental Aircraft Association International Fly-In

Indian Summer Festival in Milwaukee Native American tribes from around the country participate in this September festival. Singing, dancing, drumming, seeing colorful costumes, and basket weaving are some of the highlights.

Indian Summer Festival

Watermelon Seed-Spitting and Speed-Eating Championship Visitors bring their appetites to Pardeeville in September so they can participate in this national competition. Contestants can try to beat the current record: 2.5 pounds of watermelon in 3.5 seconds.

Laura Ingalls Wilder Days Visitors travel back in time to the mid-1800s when visiting Pepin for this September event. Visitors can see performances of the stories and songs from the Little House books, as well as blacksmiths, ironworkers, and weavers dressed in period costumes.

Oktoberfest La Crosse hosts this annual celebration in September and October. Visitors can taste ethnic foods, ride a carnival ride, and listen to German music.

Display of 6,000 Santas From November to January, visitors can see the amazing collection of life-size Santas at the House on the Rock in Spring Green. The house is decorated for the holidays, which makes visiting a perfect way to get into the spirit of Christmas.

STATE STARS

Shirley Abrahamson (1933–   ), a lawyer, was the first woman to serve as chief justice of the Wisconsin Supreme Court.

Stephen Moulton Babcock (1843–1931) taught at the University of Wisconsin. He was a chemist who developed a test that determines the amount of butterfat in dairy products.

John Bardeen (1908–1991) was a physicist born in Madison. He earned many awards during his sixty-year career and was still publishing scientific papers at the age of eighty-three. He shared the Nobel Prize in Physics in 1956 with Walter H. Brattain and William Shockley for performing research that led to the invention of the transistor. In 1972 he shared the Nobel Prize with L. N. Cooper and J. R. Schrieffer for developing the theory of superconductivity.

Ada Deer (1935–   ) won national recognition for her work in making the Menominee a federally recognized tribe and therefore keeping their reservation. She was born on the Menominee Indian Reservation in Wisconsin and teaches Native American Studies at the University of Wisconsin in Madison.

Edna Ferber (1885–1968) began her writing career at age seventeen as a newspaper reporter in Appleton. Her novels and plays contain accurate portrayals of American life in the 1920s and 1930s. Her novel *So Big* won the Pulitzer Prize in 1925, and *Show Boat* became a popular musical stage play. Ferber was hailed as the greatest woman novelist of her time.

Zona Gale (1874–1938) was born in Portage. She used her writing to argue for gender and racial equality. Her novel *Miss Lulu Bett* won the 1921 Pulitzer Prize for Drama, which made Gale the first woman to win the prize.

Cordelia Harvey (1824–1895) was called the "Wisconsin Angel" because she nursed so many hospitalized Civil War soldiers.

Edna Ferber

Woodrow Charles (Woody) Herman (1913–1987) was a famous jazz musician and bandleader who was born in Milwaukee. He founded a band, the Woody Herman Orchestra, which played a style of music that excited both musicians and nonmusicians.

Harry Houdini (1874–1926) grew up in Appleton. Born Ehrich Weiss in Hungary, he was one of the most famous escape artists of all time.

Vince Lombardi (1913–1970) coached the Green Bay Packers from 1959 to 1968. The Packers won five league titles and two Super Bowl championships under this beloved coach's leadership.

Joseph Raymond McCarthy (1908–1957) was born in Grand Chute. As a Republican U.S. senator, he led a harsh crusade against individuals he believed were supporters of communism. Eventually, he was censured by the U.S. Senate for misconduct.

Golda Meir (1893–1978) was born in Kiev, Russia, but grew up in Milwaukee. In 1921 she immigrated to Palestine, which is now Israel, where she became a great leader. She served as foreign minister from 1956 to 1965. During this time she worked with cooperative planning programs between Israel and Africa. In 1969 the Labor Party nominated Golda Meir to be prime minister, a position she held until she retired from political life in 1974. She is still recognized and respected for her dedication to her country and concern for people.

Harry Houdini

William L. (Billy) Mitchell (1879–1936) learned to fly from Orville Wright. Although he successfully commanded large air forces during World War I, he was demoted because he criticized military officials and later resigned from the military.

John Muir (1838–1914) was an explorer and naturalist who was born in Dunbar, Scotland. His family later moved to Portage, Wisconsin. Muir loved nature and saw beauty in the smallest wonders of the natural world. He had little formal schooling but was always learning new things and developing new interests. His first wilderness adventure was a 1,000-mile walk from Louisville, Kentucky, to Savannah, Georgia. Love of nature and concern for its preservation led him to found, with Robert Underwood Johnson, the Sierra Club.

Georgia O'Keeffe (1887–1986) is well known for her paintings of nature. She was born in Sun Prairie but moved to west Texas as a young adult, where she first taught art in the Amarillo public schools and later at West Texas State University. The desert landscapes of the Southwest inspired her; its influence is seen in her many paintings. She married the photographer Alfred Stieglitz and eventually settled near Taos, New Mexico, in 1949.

William Hubbs Rehnquist (1924–2005), born in Milwaukee, was appointed chief justice of the U.S. Supreme Court in 1986 by President Ronald Reagan. He was against the death penalty and believed it is constitutional to exclude women from the military draft.

Georgia O'Keeffe

Ringling Brothers Albert (1852–1916), **William H. Otto** (1858–1911), **Alfred T.** (1861–1919), **Charles** (1863–1926), and **John** (1866–1936) operated a touring circus before establishing the Ringling Brothers Circus in 1884. When the brothers bought the Barnum and Bailey Circus in 1907, theirs became the leading circus in the country. They were born in Baraboo.

Margarethe Schurz (1833–1876) was a teacher who opened the first kindergarten in the United States, in Watertown in 1856.

(George) Orson Welles (1915–1985) was born in Kenosha. An influential actor and director known for his artistic independence, he earned a reputation as a brilliant director while in his early twenties. His first film, *Citizen Kane*, is considered one of the most important films in motion picture history; it is highly regarded for its innovative camera and sound techniques. The radio drama *War of the Worlds*, in which Welles performed, realistically portrayed a martian invasion.

Frank Lloyd Wright (1867–1959) was one of this country's most influential architects. He built his own home, which he called Taliesen, in Spring Green, Wisconsin. His style was known as "organic architecture" because the buildings were designed to reflect their natural surroundings.

TOUR THE STATE

The Logging Museum (Rhinelander) This reproduction of a logging camp features a bunkhouse, a blacksmith's house, a sawmill, and displays of logging equipment.

(George)Orson Welles

Circle M Corral (Minocqua) This amusement park offers go-carts, bumper boats, horseback riding, video games, and miniature golf.

Aqualand Wildlife Park (Boulder Junction) This natural reserve has a petting zoo for children, and visitors can see most of Wisconsin's wildlife on display.

Green Bay Packers Hall of Fame (Green Bay) Visitors can view the history of one of the NFL's most successful teams and see the trophy from their first Super Bowl victory. Pictures, uniforms, equipment, and hands-on exhibits highlight the displays.

National Railroad Museum (Green Bay) Visitors can see exhibits from the steam and diesel eras, General Eisenhower's staff train, and a "Big Boy" steam locomotive.

Oshkosh B'Gosh, Inc. (Oshkosh) Visitors can take a free tour of the factory where some of America's best-known children's clothes are made.

Indian Mound Park (Sheboygan) These mounds are believed to have been built between 700 and 1000 C.E. By walking the hiking trail, visitors can see a dozen burial grounds.

Milwaukee Art Museum (Milwaukee) The museum's collection features European and American art of the nineteenth and twentieth centuries. Visitors can see works by Edgar Degas, Picasso, Georgia O'Keeffe, and Andy Warhol.

Green Bay Packers Hall of Fame

Milwaukee Art Museum

Milwaukee County Historical Society (Milwaukee) The museum contains temporary and permanent exhibits on the history of Wisconsin. Photographs show how Milwaukee has grown in the last century.

Milwaukee Public Museum (Milwaukee) This building houses the fourth-largest natural history exhibit in the United States. Visitors can walk through a rain forest exhibit and see dinosaur skeletons.

Allen-Bradley Tower Clock (Milwaukee) This landmark is in the *Guinness Book of World Records* as the largest four-faced clock in the world. Ship captains sometimes use the clock as a reference point.

Bodamer Log Cabin Historical Landmark (Milwaukee) This is a wonderful example of the log cabins built in the 1830s. It was the first log cabin built in Greenfield, Wisconsin. After layers of plaster, laths, and siding were removed, the logs were found to be in great condition.

Henry Vilas Zoo (Madison) Although this is a fun destination any time of year, visitors can ride a camel during the summer months. All year round they can pet and feed the animals at the children's zoo. This is one of the city's most popular family attractions.

Circus World Museum (Baraboo) Here visitors can see displays of circus equipment from all over the country. They can also view some of the items used by the Ringling Brothers when they started their circus in 1884.

Myrick Park Zoo (La Crosse) Here visitors will find a small collection of domestic and wild animals. Visitors can enjoy picnic areas, a wading pool, and a nature trail.

Paul Bunyan Logging Camp (Eau Claire) Visitors are greeted by a statue of the fictional lumberjack and his faithful ox, Babe. The museum has exhibits such as a cook shanty, a bunkhouse, and a blacksmith's shop.

FUN FACTS

Wisconsin is not called the Badger State because a great number of these fierce animals live in the area. The state earned its nickname because lead miners lived in dugouts similar to those made by badgers.

The first kindergarten in the United States opened in 1856 in Watertown.

William Horlick invented malted milk in 1887 in Racine.

Find Out More

BOOKS

For more information about Wisconsin, its history, and its people, check out the following books from your school or public library:

Anderson, William. *Prairie Girl, The Story of Laura Ingalls Wilder.* New York: HarperCollins, 2004.

Godfrey, Linda S., and Richard D. Hendricks. *Weird Wisconsin: Your Travel Guide to Wisconsin's Local Legends and Best Kept Secrets* (Weird). New York: Sterling, 2005.

Ling, Bettina. *Wisconsin.* Danbury, CT: Children's Press, 2002.

Lloyd, Tanya, *Wisconsin* (The America Series). Vancouver, BC: Whitccap Books, 2001.

Morgan, John, and Ellen Morgan. *50 Hikes in Wisconsin: Short and Long Loop Trails throughout the Badger State.* Woodstock, VT: Countryman Press, 2004.

Tekiela, Stan. *Mammals of Wisconsin Field Guide.* Cambridge, MN: Adventure Publications, 2005.

————. *Birds of Wisconsin Field Guide.* Cambridge, MN: Adventure Publications, 2004.

————. *Reptiles and Amphibians of Wisconsin Field Guide.* Cambridge, MN: Adventure Publications, 2004.

The State of Wisconsin Web Site (Kids Page)

http://www.wisconsin.gov/state/core/kids_page.html

Kids can learn all about Wisconsin by playing games, reading about state
trivia, and following links for more information.

Get Travel Information (maps and more)

http://www.travelwisconsin.com/placestogo/maps.htm

This site provides maps, guidebooks, and planners for visiting Wisconsin.

Interesting Wisconsin Facts and Figures

http://www.enchantedlearning.com/usa/states/wisconsin/

Visit this site to find fast facts about Wisconsin.

Wisconsin Historical Society

http://www.wisconsinhistory.org/

This site provides information on the history of Wisconsin as well as information on museums, genealogy, and historic buildings.

Wisconsin Native American People

http://www.wisconsin.gov/state/core/wisconsin_native_american_tribes.html

This page lists the Native American tribes of Wisconsin and provides links
to their respective Web pages.

Index

Page numbers in **boldface** are illustrations and charts.

Karen Zeinert was a former social studies teacher. Her articles have been published in children's magazines such as *Cricket* and *Cobblestone,* and she wrote a number of books for young people on historical subjects.

Joyce Hart has driven across the United States over twenty times and passed through Wisconsin at least ten of those times. Each time she has wandered through Wisconsin, she has been surprised by the natural beauty of the land and the friendliness of the people. She once lived in Chicago and would escape that noisy city by going to the more relaxing landscape of Wisconsin on weekends. Now Joyce lives outside Seattle, where she writes and edits books for students and takes daily hikes through a rain forest with her dog, Molly.